Southern Living®
Cookbook
Library

The
Meats
Cookbook

Copyright © 1971 Oxmoor House, Inc.
All rights reserved.
Library of Congress Catalog Number: 76-42145
ISBN: 0-8487-0329-4

Cover: Deviled Pot Roast (page 54)
Left: Stuffed Pork Chops (page 80)

contents

preface

Meats — ham, beef, veal, pork, lamb, even game and specialty meats — the core of family meals! It's exciting to prepare meats in different ways. But occasionally all of us run short of ideas. Then don't we wish they would invent a new animal!

Southern Living hasn't invented a new animal, but they've done the next best thing. They have compiled here, in one volume, the secrets of hundreds of Southern homemakers . . . favorite and cherished recipes for preparing delicious meat treats.

Southern cooking is a very special way of preparing food. It is the meat-and-potatoes goodness of Appalachia . . . the sharply-flavored Creole cooking of Louisiana . . . the Spanish-influenced cuisine of Texas. Like the South itself, Southern cooking is infinitely varied.

The SOUTHERN LIVING MEATS COOKBOOK reflects this variety in its recipes. Browsing through the pages of this book is like taking a tour through the kitchens of the South's finest cooks . . . cooks who have carefully home-tested and then signed each recipe you will find. This is a book as certain to be cherished by you as the recipes are by the women who submitted them for publication. From our kitchens to yours, welcome to the wonderful world of meats — Southern style!

terms & definitions

Barbecue . . . . To cook or grill over charcoal using a highly seasoned sauce

Baste . . . . To moisten meats with melted fat, meat drippings, fruit juice, or sauce during cooking to prevent drying and to add flavor

Bone. . . . . To remove the bones from a piece of meat

Bouillon . . . . A clear seasoned soup, usually made from beef stock

Braise . . . . To brown in fat then cook slowly, covered, in a small amount of liquid

Bread . . . . To coat with crumbs

Broil. . . . . To cook quickly by direct heat

Broth . . . . A thin soup, or the liquid in which food was cooked

Croquette. . . . . Finely ground, cooked meat which is shaped, coated, and deep-fat fried

Cube. . . . . To cut into 1 to 2-inch square pieces

Dice . . . . To cut into cubes, about 1/4 inch in size

Disjoint. . . . . To cut meat into serving pieces by separating at the joints

Dredge . . . . To dip in or coat with flour

Drippings . . . . The fat and juices collected in a roasting pan or skillet

6

Filet or Fillet	A special cut or slice of boneless meat
Glaze	To coat with a thin sweet sauce, syrup, or aspic
Lard	To insert or place strips of fat on surface for flavor and moisture
Marinate	To let stand in a mixture of oil and vinegar or lemon juice to flavor and tenderize
Panbroil	To cook in a skillet kept dry by pouring off accumulated fat
Panfry	To cook in a small amount of fat in a skillet
Parboil	To precook or boil in water until partially cooked
Piquant	Agreeably sharp in taste
Poach	To cook gently, just below the boiling point, in liquid to cover
Pot Roast	To cover and cook slowly by moist heat
Potage	Soup
Pungent	Tartly appealing to the appetite
Ragout	A thick stew of well-seasoned meat and vegetables
Roast	To cook, uncovered, in the oven by dry heat
Roux	A smooth blend of fat and flour cooked over low heat used for thickening
Saute	To fry lightly in a small amount of fat
Savoureux	Savory, tasty, tangy
Score	To make shallow cuts in surface or edges of meat
Sear	To brown quickly to seal in juices
Simmer	To cook by moist heat at temperature below boiling
Skewer	A wooden or metal pin which holds small pieces of meat and vegetables in place for roasting
Stew	To cook slowly in liquid
Stock	The liquid in which meat has been cooked
Suet	The firm white fat of beef
Truss	To fasten together with strings or skewers

It is easy to serve any cut of meat so that it is flavorful, tender, and juicy —
if that meat is cooked properly.

Broiling, roasting, and panfrying are known as the dry-heat methods of
cooking. They are used with tender cuts of meat — steak, chops, etc.

Braising and cooking in liquid are the moist-heat methods and are used
with tougher cuts of meat. Moist heat creates steam which softens the tough
connective tissues in this more sinewy meat.

BROILING

Tender, thick beef steaks, pork and lamb chops, sliced ham, and bacon are
delicious when broiled. For best results, steaks and chops should be 1 inch
thick; ham slices, 1/2 inch thick. The broiler may be preheated if desired.

cooking methods
FOR MEATS

Steaks and chops 1 1/2 inches to 2 inches thick should be at least 3 inches
from the heat. Those meats 1 inch thick or less should be placed about 2
inches from the heat.

When the top side is brown, season it as desired and turn. Ham and bacon
do not need seasoning, but steaks and chops brown better if they are seasoned
after they have been broiled. When the second side of the meat is done,
season it, and place it on a heated platter. The heated platter helps retain the
meat's heat; broiled meat cools very quickly and tastes best if it is served
piping hot.

ROASTING

In roasting, the rule of slow heat applies — the oven should be set between
300 degrees F and 325 degrees F. Chunky, juicy, tender cuts of top quality
beef, veal, pork, ham, lamb, and mutton make the very finest roasts. A roast
should weigh at least 3 to 4 pounds, but for best results should be 5 pounds
or more. If desired, the meat may be seasoned with salt and pepper. However,
this seasoning will only penetrate 1/4 inch to 1/2 inch into the roast. Place
the meat — fat side up — on a rack in an open shallow roasting pan.

Insert a meat thermometer so the bulb is in the center of the largest part
of the meat. *A meat thermometer is the only foolproof way to tell if a roast
is cooked to the desired temperature.* Do not take the roast out of the oven
to read the meat thermometer: a household meat thermometer will indicate
an accurate reading only when it is read inside a heated oven.

Do not add water, and do not cover. Do not sprinkle the meat with flour
— it will brown naturally as it cooks. Do not open the oven door to baste;

as the fat on a roast melts, it bastes itself. (This is why the meat is cooked fat side up.)

When the meat thermometer indicates the desired temperature, remove the roast from the oven. Allow the roast to set for 15 minutes after it is removed from the oven.

PANFRYING

Deep-Fat Fry: Use a deep kettle and a frying basket. Add enough fat to completely cover the meat. Heat fat to frying temperature (300 to 350 degrees F). Using the frying basket, lower a few uniform pieces of meat at a time into the hot fat. Brown meat and cook it through. When it is done, raise the basket and allow the fat to drain into the kettle. If you wish to reuse your fat, strain it through a cloth and cool. Cover and store in refrigerator.

Panfry: Use a heavy frying pan; it will ensure uniform cooking. Brown meat in a small amount of fat. Season with salt and pepper. Cook at a moderate temperature until done, turning occasionally. When turning, use tongs so that the meat will not be pierced and the juices lost. Do not cover meat while cooking.

BRAISING

Meat to be braised may be dredged with flour, then slowly browned on both sides in a small amount of fat in a heavy cooking pan with a tight cover. Season with salt, pepper, herbs, and spices. Vegetables may be added during the cooking process, and will take about 40 minutes to cook. Some of the less-tender cuts of meat may need some liquid added. Cover tightly and cook at a low temperature until tender. During cooking, the liquid should simmer but not boil.

When done, remove the roast and vegetables, if any, to a heated platter and make gravy. The gravy is an essential part of any braised meat dish. It contains meat flavors and soluble food nutrients and should be used to accompany the meat.

COOKING IN LIQUID

Large Cuts: Meat may be browned if desired. Cover meat with stock or water. Season with salt, pepper, herbs, and spices, Vegetables may be added if desired. Cover kettle and simmer until tender. If the meat is to be served cold, let it cool, and then chill in the stock in which it was cooked. If vegetables are to be cooked with the meat, as in "boiled" dinners, add them whole or in large pieces.

Stews: Cut the meat into uniform pieces, usually 1-inch to 2-inch cubes. Brown meat cubes on all sides if a brown stew is wanted. Add just enough water, vegetable juices, or soup stock to cover the meat. Season with salt, pepper, herbs, and spices. Cover kettle tightly and simmer until meat is tender. Add vegetables to the meat about 40 minutes before the meat is done. When done, remove meat and vegetables to a pan, platter, or casserole and keep hot. To thicken the stock, use a paste made of flour and a small amount of cold water or stock. Pour hot gravy over the meat and vegetables or serve separately in a sauce boat.

Grilled Dill Steak (page 60)

beef

Beef is a staple in Southern cooking.

From the simplicity of a hamburger to the elegance of a standing rib roast, beef offers cooks an endless variety of dishes to complement any menu. And, with so many cuts of beef readily available, this popular meat can fit into a wide range of food budgets.

Inexpensive beef cuts will save you money, and will provide rich taste at a low cost. The more expensive cuts are worth splurging on — they are probably America's most popular meats. And between the two price extremes, you will find a meat case full of tempting, moderately-priced beef selections.

On the following pages, readers of *Southern Living* share with you their favorite beef recipes. Many of them have been family favorites for generations and are published here for the first time. They have all been tested in the readers' homes — with mouth-watering results.

Beef can be as Southern as barbecued roast, as all-American as ground beef steak, or can take on an international flavor in such dishes as Hungarian pot roast.

Whatever your preferences — local, regional, or international — the following recipes are for dishes which will suit every taste. And because beef is a favorite food among Southern families, these recipes hopefully will add a new variety to your menu-planning.

Beef in its many forms — roasts, steaks, ribs, or hamburger — is the great American meat. In fact, the average American consumes between 85 and 100 pounds of beef each year! Beef tastes good, is nutritious, and, thanks to modern packing and refrigeration methods, it is available year 'round.

When buying beef, homemakers know what *kind* of beef cut they need. But there can be important differences in the quality of beef cuts available. One way to determine beef quality is to look for the United States Department of Agriculture purple grading stamp. Meat packers usually will ask the USDA to inspect and rate their meat cuts. Those cuts are then stamped to indicate the USDA rating. Some meat packers prefer to do their own grading. The butcher

general directions
FOR BEEF

who prepares those cuts for sale can tell the consumer how these grades compare with the USDA ones.

The USDA ratings are based on an eight-place scale, only six of which apply to meat cuts — U. S. Prime, Choice, Good, Standard, Commercial, or Utility. These categories allow for the differences in age, sex, health, breeding, feeding, and treatment before and after slaughter — all of which affect the quality of beef produced.

U. S. Prime is the best beef. It comes from young, carefully-fed cattle. This meat is smooth and well-marbled with fat. It has an outside rim of creamy fat and is firm when you touch it. Prime beef is always tender, juicy, delicious — and expensive. It is often sold only in specialized meat markets.

U. S. Choice is a little less expensive than Prime. Most people buy this grade because it is high-quality beef with the same general characteristics as Prime but with less fat.

U. S. Good is moderately-priced beef. Beef cuts graded Good have very little fat and so are not as juicy as Prime or Choice cuts, but cooked correctly they have a delightful flavor.

U. S. Standard is mildly-flavored, very lean, tender beef. It, too, is moderately priced.

U. S. Commercial is produced from mature cattle and is not as tender as are the first four grades. It may be mistaken for Prime because it has a lot of fat marbling. However, the color is darker than that of Prime beef.

U. S. Utility has little fat and comes from mature cattle. It is usually used for ground beef, stewing meat, or pot roasts.

RETAIL BEEF CUTS AND HOW TO COOK THEM

Inside Chuck Roll | Chuck Short Ribs | Standing Rib Roast | Club Steak | Pin Bone Sirloin Steak | Round Steak | Standing Rump*

Chuck Tender | Petite Steaks* | Rib Steak | T-Bone Steak | Flat Bone Sirloin Steak | Top Round Steak* | Rolled Rump*

Blade Pot roast or Steak | Arm Pot roast or Steak | Rib Steak, Boneless | Porterhouse Steak | | | Outside (Bottom) Round Steak or Pot roast

Boneless Shoulder Pot roast or Steak | Boston Cut | Delmonico (Rib Eye) Roast or Steak | Top Loin Steak | Wedge Bone Sirloin Steak | Eye of Round | Heel of Round

Filet Mignon Tenderloin Steak (also from Sirloin 1, 2, 3) | Boneless Sirloin Steak

CHUCK Braise, Cook in Liquid | **RIB** Roast, Broil, Panbroil, Panfry | **SHORT LOIN** Roast, Broil, Panbroil, Panfry | **SIRLOIN** Roast, Broil, Panbroil, Panfry | **ROUND** Braise, Cook in Liquid

Shank Cross Cuts | Fresh Brisket | Short Ribs | Skirt Steak Fillets* | Ground Beef (Flank, Short Plate, Shank, Brisket, Rib, Chuck, Loin, Round) | Flank Steak* | Tip Steak* | Sirloin Tip*

Beef for Stew (also from other cuts) | Corned Brisket | Rolled Plate | Plate Beef | Beef Patties | Flank Steak Fillets* | Cube Steak*

FORE SHANK Braise, Cook in Liquid | **BRISKET** Braise, Cook in Liquid | **SHORT PLATE** Braise, Cook in Liquid | **GROUND BEEF** Roast, Broil, Panbroil, Panfry | **FLANK STEAK** Braise, Cook in Liquid | **TIP (KNUCKLE)** Braise, Cook in Liquid

* May be Roasted, Broiled, Panbroiled or Panfried from high quality beef.

TIMETABLE FOR COOKING BEEF

CUT	ROASTED AT 300 F. OVEN TEMPERATURE		BROILED		BRAISED	COOKED IN LIQUID
	Meat Thermometer Reading Degrees F.	Time Minutes per lb.	Meat Thermometer Reading Degrees F.	Total Time Minutes	Total Time Hours	Total Time Hours
Standing Ribs	140 (rare)	18 to 20				
Standing Ribs	160 (medium)	22 to 25				
Standing Ribs	170 (well)	27 to 30				
Rolled Ribs	Same as above	Add 10 to 15				
Blade, 3rd to 5th Rib (high quality only)	150-170	25 to 30				
Rump (high quality only)	150-170	25 to 30				
Tenderloin	140-170	20 to 25				
Beef Loaf	160-170	25 to 30				
Steaks (1 inch)			140 (rare) 160 (medium)	15 to 20 20 to 30		
Steaks (1 1/2 inch)			140 (rare) 160 (medium	25 to 35 35 to 50		
Steaks (2 inch)			140 (rare) 160 (medium)	30 to 40 50 to 70		
Beef Patties (1 inch)			140 (rare) 160 (medium)	12 to 15 18 to 20		
Pot-Roasts						
Arm or Blade					3 to 4	
Rump					3 to 4	
Swiss Steak					2 to 3	
Corned Beef						3 1/2 to 5
Fresh Beef					3 to 4	3 to 4
Stew						2 to 3

BEEF STROGANOFF SALAD

2 c. coarsely ground roast beef	2 tsp. horseradish
1 c. sour cream	2 tbsp. chili sauce
6 tbsp. pickle relish	1 1/2 tsp. salt
1/2 c. minced onion	

Combine all ingredients in a mixing bowl and mix well. Refrigerate until chilled. Serve on lettuce. 3 cups.

Mrs. Lee Tschirhart, Castroville, Texas

SALCOM

3 lb. round steak or stew beef	1 can tomatoes, drained
1 lge. bell pepper	Dash of ground red pepper
4 stalks celery	Mayonnaise
1 lge. onion	

Cook the steak in boiling, salted water until tender, drain and cool. Reserve 1/2 cup beef stock. Grind steak fine. Grind the bell pepper, celery and onion and add to steak. Chop tomatoes and add to steak mixture. Add the red pepper and reserved beef stock and mix well. Add enough mayonnaise to moisten. Place in salad bowl and garnish with green pepper rings or onion rings.

Mrs. Edgar J. Maxwell, Lexington, Georgia

BEEF-BEAN SALAD

1 lb. hamburger	1/2 tsp. hot sauce
1 can tomatoes, drained	1/2 15-oz. can refried beans
1 c. shredded Velveeta cheese	6 oz. corn chips
2 heads lettuce, shredded	Salt and pepper to taste
1/2 c. chopped green onions	

Cook the hamburger in a skillet until brown. Drain and reserve fat. Place the hamburger in a salad bowl. Drain the tomatoes and reserve juice. Chop tomatoes and add to hamburger. Add the cheese, lettuce and onions and toss lightly. Place the reserved fat, reserved juice, hot sauce and refried beans in a saucepan and heat through. Add to hamburger mixture and toss. Add corn chips and season with salt and pepper. 12 servings.

Mrs. D. T. Kirkland, Baton Rouge, Louisiana

MAIN DISH SALAD

2 c. cooked beef, cut in strips	2 tbsp. sliced sweet pickle
1 No. 2 can kidney beans, drained	1/4 c. mayonnaise
1 c. chopped celery	1 tbsp. chili sauce
1/4 c. chopped onion	1 tsp. salt
2 hard-cooked eggs, chopped	1 head lettuce

Combine the beef, beans, celery, onion, eggs, pickle, mayonnaise, chili sauce and salt in a bowl and toss lightly. Cover and chill for 30 minutes. Serve in lettuce cups. 4-6 servings.

Mrs. Aline Wilson, Ringgold, Louisiana

COACH HOUSE PLATTER

2 15-oz. cans red kidney beans	2 tbsp. capers
1 4-oz. can whole mushrooms	1/2 tsp. salt
1 12-oz. can whole kernel corn	1/4 tsp. pepper
1 4-oz. can pimentos	2/3 c. Cheddar and wine dressing
1 1/2 c. diagonally sliced celery	12 slices cold roast beef
2 tbsp. finely chopped onion	Salad greens
1/4 c. finely chopped parsley	

Drain the kidney beans, mushrooms, corn and pimentos and cut the pimentos in strips. Combine the celery, kidney beans, mushrooms, corn, onion, half the pimento strips, 2 tablespoons parsley and 1 tablespoon capers in a mixing bowl and sprinkle with salt and pepper. Add the dressing and toss to mix well. Chill. Fold slices of roast beef and arrange along sides of a serving platter. Place salad greens at ends of platter and spoon the corn mixture in mound in center. Garnish with remaining pimento strips, parsley and capers. 6 servings.

Coach House Platter (above)

BLENDER BEEF SALAD

1 lb. boneless stew beef	1/4 tsp. pepper
3 hard-cooked eggs	Salt to taste
1 onion	1/2 c. mayonnaise
1 clove of garlic	6 lettuce leaves
1/2 c. chopped celery	

Cook the stew beef in boiling, salted water until tender, drain and cool. Place the beef in a blender container, small amount at a time, and blend until ground. Blend the eggs, onion, garlic and celery in the blender and add to beef. Add the pepper, salt and mayonnaise and mix well. Serve on lettuce. 6 servings.

Mrs. T. P. Ferguson, Biloxi, Mississippi

SALAD CON CARNE

1 lb. ground beef	1/2 sm. onion, sliced into rings
1/4 c. chopped onion	1/4 c. green pepper, cut in strips
1 tbsp. beef gravy base	1/2 c. sliced ripe olives
6 drops of hot pepper sauce	1/4 lb. shredded sharp Cheddar
1 tsp. cornstarch	cheese
1 med. head lettuce	1 6-oz. package corn chips,
1 lge. tomato, cut in wedges	crushed

Brown the beef in a skillet and add the chopped onion, gravy base and pepper sauce. Stir in 3/4 cup water and mix well. Simmer for 10 minutes, stirring frequently. Combine the cornstarch and 1 tablespoon water and stir into beef mixture. Cook, stirring, until thickened. Tear the lettuce into bite-sized pieces and place in a salad bowl. Add the tomato, sliced onion, green pepper, olives and cheese and toss well. Spoon beef mixture on top and sprinkle with corn chips. 4-6 servings.

Judy Dunn, Bulane, Kentucky

HENRY VIII SALAD BOWL

1 head romaine	1 c. chili sauce
1 bunch chicory	1 tbsp. grated onion
1 bunch escarole	1/2 dill pickle, diced
Thin ham strips	1 clove of garlic, mashed
Roast beef strips	1 tbsp. parsley
Swiss cheese strips	1/2 tsp. salt
1 c. olive oil	1/2 tsp. sugar
1 c. wine vinegar	Ground pepper to taste
1 c. catsup	

Tear the romaine, chicory and escarole into bite-sized pieces and place in a large salad bowl. Add desired amounts of ham, roast beef and Swiss cheese. Combine remaining ingredients and mix well. Pour over the romaine mixture and toss well. Garnish with peeled and quartered tomatoes and hard-cooked eggs.

Mrs. W. A. Giberson, Brunswick, Georgia

MEXICALI MEAT PIE

6 slices bacon	1 tsp. salt
1 c. all-purpose flour	1/8 tsp. pepper
6 tbsp. cornmeal	1 8-oz. can tomato sauce
3 to 4 tbsp. cold water	1 egg, beaten
1 lb. ground beef	1/4 c. milk
1 8-oz. can whole kernel corn	1/2 tsp. dry mustard
1/4 c. finely chopped green pepper	1/2 tsp. Worcestershire sauce
1/4 c. finely chopped onion	1 1/2 c. grated Cheddar cheese
1/2 tsp. oregano	4 stuffed olives, sliced
1/2 tsp. chili powder	

Fry the bacon in a skillet until crisp, remove from skillet and break into large pieces. Pour bacon drippings from skillet, reserve 1/3 cup and chill until firm. Combine the flour and 2 tablespoons cornmeal in a mixing bowl. Cut in reserved bacon drippings until mixture is the size of small peas. Stir in the water gradually until pastry is just moist enough to hold together. Form into a ball and roll out on a floured surface to a circle 1 1/2 inches larger than an inverted 9-inch pie pan. Fit into pie pan, then fold edge under and flute. Brown the ground beef in a large skillet and drain off excess fat. Drain the corn and add to ground beef. Add the green pepper, onion, remaining cornmeal, oregano, chili powder, 1/2 teaspoon salt, pepper and tomato sauce and mix well. Place in pastry-lined pie pan. Bake at 425 degrees for 25 minutes. Combine the egg, milk, remaining salt, mustard, Worcestershire sauce and cheese and mix well. Spread on beef mixture. Top with the bacon and olives and bake for 5 minutes longer or until cheese melts. Remove from oven and let stand for 10 minutes before serving. May be served with tomato sauce, if desired. 6 servings.

Mexicali Meat Pie (above)

GRAND-STYLE GROUND BEEF

1 1/2 lb. ground beef	1 tsp. salt
1 c. chopped onion	1/4 c. catsup
1 8-oz. package cream cheese	1 can refrigerator biscuits
1 can cream of mushroom soup	1/2 c. sliced stuffed olives (opt.)
1/4 c. milk	

Brown the ground beef and onion in a skillet and drain. Soften the cream cheese, then stir in the soup and milk. Add the salt, catsup and beef mixture and pour into a 2-quart casserole. Place biscuits around edge of the casserole and place slices of olive in center of each biscuit. Bake at 375 degrees for 15 to 20 minutes or until golden brown.

Mrs. Joseph R. Kyzar, Nashville, Tennessee

CHILI POTPIE

3 tbsp. onion flakes	3/4 c. cornmeal
3 tbsp. water	1/4 c. flour
1 1/2 lb. ground beef, crumbled	1 1/2 tbsp. baking powder
1 tsp. garlic salt	1 egg, beaten
1/2 c. chopped bell pepper	1/2 c. milk
1 8-oz. can tomato sauce	1/4 c. bacon drippings
1 1-lb. can tomatoes	1 tbsp. parsley
1 20-oz. can ranch-style beans	1/4 c. grated cheese
1 tbsp. chili powder	Paprika
1 1/2 tsp. salt	

Combine the onion flakes and water in a small bowl. Saute the beef until partially done. Add the onion, garlic salt and bell pepper and cook until brown. Add the tomato sauce, tomatoes, beans, chili powder and 1 teaspoon salt and simmer for 10 minutes. Sift the cornmeal, flour, remaining salt and baking powder together into a mixing bowl. Add the egg, milk and bacon drippings and stir until smooth. Stir in parsley. Pour the beef mixture into a shallow baking dish and sprinkle with cheese. Spoon cornmeal mixture around edge of baking dish and sprinkle with paprika. Bake at 400 degrees for 15 minutes.

Mrs. J. T. Springer, Lenorah, Texas

SOUTHERN MEAT-PIE

1 1/4 c. flour	3 tbsp. water
3/4 c. cornmeal	1 lb. ground beef
1 3/4 tsp. salt	1/2 c. chopped onions
Shortening	1 1/2 tsp. chili powder
Evaporated milk	1 can vegetable soup

Sift flour, cornmeal and 1 teaspoon salt together into a mixing bowl and cut in 1/2 cup shortening. Combine 6 tablespoons milk and water and stir into the flour mixture. Roll out 3/4 of the pastry on a floured board and line a pie pan. Bake at 425 degrees for 10 minutes. Brown the ground beef and onions over low heat in 3 tablespoons shortening. Add the chili powder, remaining salt and soup and mix thoroughly. Remove from heat. Add 3/4 cup milk and pour into baked crust. Roll out remaining pastry, cut in strips and place over pie crisscross fashion. Bake for 15 minutes longer or until brown. 4-6 servings.

Mrs. Gwen Zimmerman, Zachary, Louisiana

HOLIDAY EGG NOODLES AND HAMBURGERS

1 egg, beaten	3/4 c. finely chopped scallions
1 tbsp. cold water	1/4 c. finely chopped parsley
2 tsp. prepared mustard	1/4 c. margarine
Salt	2 c. diced green peppers
Pepper	1/4 c. diced pimentos
1 lb. ground chuck	3 qt. boiling water
1/4 c. grated Parmesan cheese	4 c. wide egg noodles

Combine the egg, cold water, mustard, 1 teaspoon salt and 1/8 teaspoon pepper in a large bowl. Add the ground chuck, Parmesan cheese, 1/4 cup scallions and parsley and toss lightly until combined. Shape into patties and place in a shallow baking pan. Broil until brown on both sides and keep warm. Melt the margarine in a large skillet over medium heat, add the green pepper and remaining scallions and saute for 6 to 8 minutes or until tender. Stir in the pimentos. Add 1 tablespoon salt to boiling water in a saucepan and add noodles gradually so that water continues to boil. Cook, stirring occasionally, until tender and drain. Toss noodles with vegetable mixture and season to taste with salt and pepper. Turn into a serving dish and top with Holiday Hamburgers. 4 servings.

Holiday Egg Noodles and Hamburgers (above)

BARBECUED HAMBURGERS

1 lb. ground beef	1/3 c. dill pickle juice
1 tbsp. minced onion	1/3 c. chili sauce
1/2 c. dry bread crumbs	2 tsp. Worcestershire sauce
1/2 c. milk	3 tsp. diced dill pickles
1 egg, beaten	2 drops of hot sauce
1/2 tsp. salt	

Combine first 5 ingredients with 1/4 teaspoon salt and mix well. Shape into patties. Brown in a skillet on both sides, then place in a baking pan. Mix remaining salt with remaining ingredients thoroughly and pour over patties. Bake at 375 degrees for 25 minutes.

Mrs. Edna Goundie, Childress, Texas

SCOTCH MEAT PATTIES

3/4 lb. ground beef	1 c. water
1/3 c. milk	1/4 c. chopped celery
3/4 c. quick-cooking oats	1/4 c. chopped green pepper
Salt	1/4 c. chopped onion
Pepper to taste	1 tsp. Worcestershire sauce
2 tbsp. fat or oil	1 tbsp. flour

Combine the beef, milk, oats, 1 teaspoon salt and pepper and shape into thin patties. Brown on both sides in fat in a frypan. Add the water, vegetables, Worcestershire sauce, salt to taste and pepper and cover. Cook over low heat for 30 minutes. Blend flour with 1 tablespoon cold water and stir into the celery mixture. Cook until thickened, stirring occasionally.

Mrs. R. J. Barnes, Mine Run, Virginia

HERO HAMBURGERS

2 lb. ground beef	1/2 lb. American cheese, grated
2 eggs, slightly beaten	1 sm. jar pickle relish
1/2 tsp. salt	1/4 c. chopped onion
1 c. barbecue sauce	8 hamburger rolls, split

Combine the beef, eggs, salt and 1/4 cup barbecue sauce and mix lightly. Shape into 16 patties. Place about 1 teaspoon each cheese, pickle relish, onion and barbecue sauce on top of 8 patties and cover with remaining patties. Press edges together to seal and place in a shallow baking pan. Broil for about 5 minutes on each side, basting with remaining barbecue sauce. Serve in heated hamburger rolls. 8 servings.

Mrs. John Earl Kersh, Jackson, Mississippi

POTATOBURGERS

2 c. grated potatoes	2 tbsp. chopped onions
1 lb. ground beef	3 tbsp. chopped green peppers

1 1/2 tsp. salt
1/8 tsp. pepper
2 tbsp. butter

2 tbsp. flour
1 c. milk

Combine first 6 ingredients and shape into 6 patties. Fry in butter in a skillet over medium heat for 12 to 15 minutes on each side or until brown. Remove patties from skillet and keep hot. Add the flour to skillet drippings and blend well. Add the milk and cook until smooth and thickened, stirring constantly. Season to taste with additional salt and pepper and serve over Potatoburgers. 6 servings.

Mrs. Dollie W. Presley, Council, Virginia

HAMBURGERS WITH SPANISH OLIVE RELISH

2 tbsp. olive or salad oil
1 c. coarsely chopped onion
1 c. diced green pepper
1 sm. clove of garlic, crushed
1/2 tsp. paprika

1/2 c. sliced stuffed olives
1/2 tsp. basil leaves
1 lb. ground chuck
1 tsp. salt
1/8 tsp. pepper

Heat the oil in a large skillet. Add the onion, green pepper, garlic and paprika and saute over medium heat until green pepper is tender. Stir in the olives and basil leaves, remove from skillet and keep warm. Mix the ground chuck with salt and pepper and shape into 6 patties. Fry patties in same skillet until browned. Spoon the olive mixture on hamburgers and heat through. Serve on hamburger buns or hard rolls, if desired.

Hamburgers with Spanish Olive Relish (above)

Mayan Casserole (below)

MAYAN CASSEROLE

1 lb. ground beef	1 8-oz. can whole kernel corn
2 tbsp. olive or salad oil	1/4 c. chopped parsley
1 c. chopped onion	2 tsp. chili powder
1 clove of garlic, minced	1 tsp. salt
1 1-lb. can cut Blue Lake	1 bouillon cube, crumbled
green beans	4 c. large corn chips
2 8-oz. cans tomato sauce	1 c. grated Cheddar cheese

Brown the ground beef in oil in a skillet. Add the onion and garlic and cook until lightly browned. Drain the beans and reserve liquid. Add enough water to reserved liquid to make 1 1/4 cups liquid and stir into beef mixture. Add the beans, tomato sauce, corn, parsley, chili powder, salt and bouillon cube and bring to a boil. Reserve several corn chips for topping. Crumble remaining corn chips and stir into hamburger mixture. Turn into a 2-quart casserole and top with ring of cheese and reserved corn chips. Bake at 350 degrees for 20 minutes. 6-8 servings.

CHALUPES

1 lb. lean ground beef	1 pkg. frozen tortillas
4 tbsp. chili powder	Salt to taste
1 tbsp. oregano	2 tomatoes, sliced
2 tbsp. garlic salt	1 head lettuce, sliced
2 No. 303 cans refried beans	2 c. grated Cheddar cheese

Cook the beef in a 3-quart saucepan until browned. Add the chili powder, oregano and garlic salt and stir until well blended. Drain off the grease into a 10-inch skillet. Add beans to the beef mixture and cook over low heat for 20 minutes. Fry tortillas until crisp in grease in skillet and drain. Salt each tortilla. Place the beef mixture in serving dishes and top each serving with tomatoes, lettuce and cheese. Serve with tortillas. 6-8 servings.

Mildred Hill, Hillsboro, Texas

BEEF TACOS

1/2 lb. ground beef	Oil
1 tsp. monosodium glutamate	12 soft tortillas
1/2 tsp. salt	Shredded lettuce
1/4 tsp. chili powder	Chopped tomatoes
1/8 tsp. garlic powder	

Season the beef with monosodium glutamate, salt, chili powder and garlic powder. Cover bottom of a skillet with 1/2 inch oil and heat. Place the beef mixture in center of tortillas and fold over. Place in small amount of hot oil and fry for 1 minute and 30 seconds on each side. Remove and drain on paper towel. Stuff remaining open space of tortillas with lettuce and tomatoes. 12 servings.

Mary L. Matl, Buckholts, Texas

ENCHILADAS

1 lb. ground beef	2 pkg. tortillas
Salt and pepper to taste	1 lb. cheese, grated
Oil	3 med. onions, finely chopped
Chili sauce	

Cook the ground beef, salt and pepper in 1 tablespoon oil in a frypan for 10 minutes, stirring frequently. Add 1 cup chili sauce and set aside. Cook the tortillas in oil in a skillet until soft. Fill each tortilla with beef mixture, cheese and onions and roll as for jelly roll. Place tortillas close together in a shallow baking pan and cover with chili sauce and remaining cheese and onions. Bake at 350 degrees until bubbly.

Mrs. Thomas W. Paul, Aransas Pass, Texas

MEXICAN CASSEROLE

1 c. chopped onions	2 cans tomato sauce
1 lb. hamburger	1/4 c. enchilada sauce
1 tsp. salt	1 can corn
1/4 tsp. oregano	12 tortillas
1/4 tsp. rosemary	1 c. grated sharp cheese
4 tbsp. salad oil	

Brown the onions, hamburger and seasonings in the oil in a skillet. Add the tomato sauce, enchilada sauce and corn and simmer for 2 minutes. Line a greased casserole with 6 tortillas and pour half the hamburger mixture over tortillas. Sprinkle with 1/2 cup cheese and repeat layers. Bake for 15 to 20 minutes at 350 degrees.

Mrs. Rita S. Miller, Foreman, Arkansas

Favorite Swedish Meatballs (below)

FAVORITE SWEDISH MEATBALLS

4 eggs, slightly beaten	1/4 tsp. cardamon (opt.)
2 c. milk	2 1/2 lb. finely ground beef
1 c. dry bread crumbs	1/4 c. flour
1 c. minced onions	3 c. beef stock
1/4 c. butter	1 c. light cream
1/4 tsp. nutmeg	Pepper to taste
1/4 tsp. allspice (opt.)	1 tsp. dillweed

Mix the eggs, milk and crumbs and let stand. Cook the onions in 2 tablespoons butter in a skillet until tender. Remove onions with a slotted spoon and add to the crumb mixture. Add 3 teaspoons salt, spices and beef and mix thoroughly. Chill for 1 hour to blend flavors, then shape into 1-inch balls. Melt remaining butter in the skillet and brown the meatballs over low heat, turning carefully so meatballs will hold shape. Place in a Dutch oven. Add the flour to drippings in skillet and blend. Cook until flour browns. Add beef broth and cook, stirring, until smooth and thickened. Add the cream, salt to taste, pepper and dillweed. Strain over meatballs and simmer, covered, over low heat for 30 minutes. May be baked at 325 degrees for 30 minutes. 10-12 servings.

MEATBALLS SAVOUREUX

3 tbsp. chopped onion	3/4 c. milk
2 tbsp. butter or margarine	1 1/2 c. soft bread crumbs

1/4 tsp. nutmeg	1 beaten egg
1/8 tsp. pepper	1 can consomme
1 1/2 tsp. salt	1 1/2 tbsp. flour
1 lb. ground beef	1 1/2 tbsp. water

Saute the onion in butter in a saucepan for 5 minutes and remove onion. Combine the milk and bread crumbs in a mixing bowl. Add nutmeg, pepper, ground beef, onions, salt and egg and mix well. Form into small balls and brown in remaining butter in the saucepan. Add the consomme and cover. Simmer for 5 minutes, then place meatballs on a platter. Blend flour and water and stir into consomme. Cook until thickened, stirring constantly, and serve with meatballs.

Mrs. Sam C. Hensley, Kingston, Tennessee

MEATBALL POÊLON DINNER

4 strips bacon, diced	1 can kidney beans
1 lb. ground beef	1 can tomato soup
1 1/2 tsp. salt	1/2 soup can water
1/4 tsp. pepper	1 tbsp. chili powder
1 med. onion, chopped	2 c. cooked macaroni
1 green pepper, cut in strips	

Saute the bacon in a large skillet until crisp and remove from skillet. Combine the ground beef with 1 teaspoon salt and pepper and shape into 20 balls. Brown in bacon fat in the skillet and remove from skillet. Saute the onion and green pepper in same skillet until tender. Add beans, soup, water, chili powder, macaroni, remaining salt and meatballs and cover. Simmer for 15 minutes and garnish with bacon. 6 servings.

Mrs. Robert Pieczyh, New Albany, Mississippi

MEATBALLS IN BUTTERMILK SAUCE

1 lb. ground beef	Butter
1/2 c. bread crumbs	1/4 c. flour
1/4 c. diced onion	2 tbsp. sugar
1/2 c. milk	1 1/2 tbsp. dry mustard
2 tsp. salt	2 1/4 c. buttermilk
1/4 tsp. pepper	1 egg, beaten

Combine the ground beef, bread crumbs, onion, milk, 1 teaspoon salt and 1/8 teaspoon pepper and mix well. Shape into 8 meatballs and brown on all sides in 3 tablespoons butter in a skillet. Remove from skillet and keep hot. Add 1/4 cup butter to drippings left in the skillet and heat until melted. Mix the flour with the sugar, mustard, remaining salt and pepper and stir into butter. Stir in the buttermilk and cook over low heat until smooth and thickened, stirring constantly. Stir some of the hot sauce into the egg. Return to mixture in skillet and cook for 2 to 3 minutes longer. Pour into a well-greased 1 1/2-quart casserole and add meatballs. Bake in 300-degree oven for 30 minutes. 4 servings.

Mrs. Will D. Martin, South Pittsburg, Tennessee

Apple-Hamburger Balls in Pastry (below)

APPLE-HAMBURGER BALLS IN PASTRY

3/4 lb. ground chuck
1 egg, beaten
2 c. canned applesauce
1 1/2 c. herb-seasoned stuffing
  mix
3/4 tsp. salt
Dash of pepper

1/2 tsp. sage
1/4 c. shortening
1 1/2 c. sliced onions
1/4 c. butter or margarine
Pastry for 2-crust pie
1 can cream of mushroom soup
1 soup can milk or water

Combine the ground chuck, egg and 1 cup applesauce. Add the stuffing mix, 1/2 teaspoon salt, pepper and sage and mix thoroughly. Form into 10 balls. Brown on all sides in shortening in a skillet and remove from skillet. Melt butter in the skillet, add onions and saute until light brown. Add remaining applesauce and salt. Roll out pastry on a floured surface and cut into 10 squares. Place an equal amount of applesauce mixture and 1 meatball on each square. Moisten edges of pastry squares with water and draw up corners over meatball. Press edges of pastry together to seal and place on baking sheet. Bake at 400 degrees for 20 to 25 minutes or until brown. Mix the soup and water in a saucepan and heat through, but do not boil. Serve with baked hamburger pastries. 5 servings.

MEATBALLS WITH PINTO BEANS

1 lb. ground beef
2 onions, chopped
1/2 c. catsup or barbecue sauce

Salt and pepper to taste
3 c. cooked pinto beans

Mix all ingredients except pinto beans and shape into medium balls. Drop into pinto beans in a saucepan and cook over medium heat until meatballs are done and liquid is thickened.

Cindy Wayt, Pryor, Oklahoma

SWEDISH MEATBALLS

1 lb. ground round steak
2 tbsp. finely chopped onion
1 tsp. salt
1/8 tsp. pepper

2 1/4 c. milk
2 eggs, slightly beaten
4 c. corn flakes

Place the ground steak in a bowl and add the onion, salt, pepper, 1 1/4 cups milk and eggs. Roll corn flakes into crumbs and add to ground steak mixture. Mix thoroughly and form into balls. Saute in butter in a skillet over low heat until brown and remove from skillet. Add remaining milk to the skillet drippings and heat through. Pour over the meatballs. 4-5 servings.

Mrs. Agness Capps, Warrenton, North Carolina

FAR EAST MEATBALLS WITH ORIENTAL SAUCE

3 slices bread, crusts removed
1 egg
2 tbsp. horseradish
1/2 tsp. salt
1 5-oz. can water chestnuts,
    chopped
1 lb. ground chuck

1/4 c. flour
2 tbsp. peanut oil
3/4 c. orange marmalade
1 clove of garlic, minced
3 tbsp. soy sauce
2 tbsp. lemon juice
1/4 c. peanut butter

Combine first 6 ingredients with 1/2 cup water and mix lightly. Form into 24 meatballs and dredge with flour. Brown in hot peanut oil in a skillet. Remove to a platter and keep warm. Drain excess fat from skillet and add remaining ingredients and 3 tablespoons water to skillet. Heat, stirring, for about 2 minutes or until bubbly. Spoon over meatballs. 4 servings.

Far East Meatballs with Oriental Sauce (above)

WILD RICE CASSEROLE

1 8-oz. box wild rice	2 bay leaves
1 med. onion, chopped	3 cans chicken with rice soup
Olive oil	3 cans mushrooms
1 1/2 lb. ground chuck	Salt and pepper to taste
1 tsp. seasoned salt	

Cover the rice with boiling water and let stand. Brown the onion in small amount of olive oil. Add the ground chuck and cook until brown, stirring constantly. Drain the rice and add to ground chuck mixture. Add remaining ingredients. Bake at 300 degrees for about 1 hour and 30 minutes or until rice is tender, stirring occasionally and adding hot water, if needed.

Mrs. A. Jude Robinson, Auburn, Alabama

SALAMAGUNDI

3/4 c. rice	1 c. chopped onion
1 1/2 tsp. salt	1/2 c. chopped green pepper
Dash of pepper	1 lb. ground beef
2 8-oz. cans seasoned tomato	1 12-oz. can whole kernel corn
sauce	2 to 3 tsp. chili powder
1 c. hot water	3 slices bacon

Place the rice, 1 teaspoon salt and pepper in a casserole and add 1 can tomato sauce and hot water. Add the onion and green pepper, then add ground beef. Sprinkle with remaining salt. Drain the corn and place over the ground beef. Mix chili powder with remaining tomato sauce and pour over corn. Top with bacon slices and cover. Bake for 1 hour at 375 degrees. Uncover and bake for 15 minutes longer or until rice is done. 5-6 servings.

Mrs. T. P. Brisley, St. Petersburg, Florida

HERBED HAMBURGER AND RICE

1 lb. hamburger, crumbled	1 No. 2 can chicken broth
2 tbsp. butter	2 c. cooked rice
2 tbsp. instant minced onion	1/8 tsp. oregano
1/2 c. chopped celery	Pinch of thyme
1/4 c. chopped parsley	Pinch of rosemary
1/4 tsp. salt	Pinch of marjoram
1/4 tsp. pepper	

Cook the hamburger in the butter until browned. Add the onion, celery and parsley and cook for 5 minutes. Add salt, pepper and chicken broth, then stir in the rice and herbs. Cook, covered, over low heat for 15 minutes and garnish with additional parsley.

Mrs. James Whitfield, Miami, Florida

SOUTHERN BEEF RING

1 c. soft bread crumbs	1/4 tsp. salt
1 slightly beaten egg	1 pkg. brown gravy mix
1/4 c. water	1/2 c. chopped celery
1/2 c. canned tomatoes	1 sm. onion, chopped
1/4 tsp. seasoned salt	1 1/2 lb. ground beef
1/2 tsp. garlic salt	

Combine first 8 ingredients and mix well. Add remaining ingredients and mix thoroughly. Form into a ring in greased shallow baking dish. Bake at 350 degrees for 1 hour or until well browned. Slide ring onto serving platter and fill center with rice. Serve with gravy. 6 servings.

Elizabeth Moore, Hartford, Alabama

SPAGHETTI PIE

2 c. cooked spaghetti	1/2 c. evaporated milk
1 onion, chopped	1 c. shredded Cheddar cheese
1/2 c. sliced mushrooms	1 tbsp. angostura bitters
1/2 c. diced celery	1 tsp. salt
3 tbsp. butter	1 tsp. prepared mustard
1 lb. ground beef	Dash of pepper
2 eggs	1/2 c. buttered bread crumbs

Arrange the spaghetti on bottom and sides of a well-buttered 1 1/2-quart casserole. Saute the onion, mushrooms and celery in a skillet in butter for 5 minutes. Add the ground beef and cook, stirring constantly, until the beef loses red color. Beat the eggs and stir in the milk, cheese, angostura bitters, salt, mustard and pepper. Combine with beef mixture and stir well. Pour into spaghetti and sprinkle with bread crumbs. Bake at 350 degrees for 35 minutes. Loosen sides with spatula, invert onto serving platter and cut into wedges. 6 servings.

Spaghetti Pie (above)

COMPANY BEEF

1 lb. lean ground beef	2 tbsp. chopped parsley
2 tbsp. shortening (opt.)	1 5-oz. package elbow macaroni
1 med. onion, chopped	Salt and pepper to taste
2 c. canned tomatoes	1 can cream of mushroom soup
1 tbsp. steak sauce	1 sm. can tomato sauce (opt.)
1/4 c. chopped green pepper	1 c. grated cheese

Brown the ground beef in heavy skillet in shortening. Add the onion, tomatoes, steak sauce, green pepper and parsley and simmer for 30 minutes. Cook macaroni according to package directions. Combine macaroni, beef mixture, salt and pepper in a casserole and mix well. Spoon in mushroom soup and tomato sauce and mix. Sprinkle cheese over top. Bake at 350 degrees for 30 minutes.

Mrs. Fred S. Robinson, Sr., Decatur, Alabama

ZAMIZETTI

2 med. onions, chopped	1 lb. ground beef
2 med. green peppers, chopped	2 garlic buds, crushed
Butter	1 can tomato soup
1 sm. package egg noodles	1/2 lb. grated cheese

Cook the onions and green peppers in small amount of butter in a saucepan until tender. Cook the noodles according to package directions and drain. Add 2 tablespoons butter and mix gently until butter is melted. Cook the ground beef in a skillet until lightly browned. Add the onion mixture, garlic and soup and mix well. Place alternate layers of noodles, beef mixture and cheese in a casserole. Bake at 375 degrees for 20 to 30 minutes or until bubbly.

Mrs. J. F. Barlow, Savannah, Tennessee

MEATBALLS ITALIANO

1 lb. lean ground beef	1/4 c. olive oil
1 1 1/2-oz. can Parmesan cheese	2 No. 2 1/2 cans Italian-style
1 c. bread crumbs, toasted	tomatoes
2 eggs	2 6-oz. cans tomato paste
2 tsp. salt	1 tsp. rosemary
1/2 tsp. pepper	1/2 tsp. thyme
2 tsp. savory	1 bay leaf
2 lge. cloves of garlic, crushed	1 tsp. oregano
2 c. chopped onions	2 4-oz. cans sliced mushrooms

Mix the ground beef, cheese, bread crumbs, eggs, 1 teaspoon salt, 1/4 teaspoon pepper and 1 teaspoon savory and shape into 1-inch balls. Fry the garlic and onions in oil in a large saucepan until golden. Add remaining salt, pepper and savory and remaining ingredients and mix well. Add the meatballs and simmer for 3 hours. Serve over thin, cooked spaghetti and top with additional Parmesan cheese. Meatballs and sauce may be frozen and reheated. 6 servings.

Robert R. Cruse, Colonial Heights, Virginia

TAGLIARINI

1 lge. onion, chopped
1 lb. ground beef
2 cans tomato soup
1 c. water
1 tsp. salt

1 can mushrooms
2 c. noodles
2 c. whole kernel corn
1 c. chopped ripe olives
1 c. grated sharp Cheddar cheese

Saute the onion and ground beef in a skillet until lightly browned and add remaining ingredients. Pour into a casserole. Bake at 350 degrees for 20 to 25 minutes. 4 servings.

Mrs. Lee Rowley, Mauldin, South Carolina

MACARONI CHILI

2 lb. ground round
3 tbsp. olive or salad oil
1   1-lb. 12-oz. can tomatoes
1 qt. tomato juice
2 c. chopped onions
3 cloves of garlic, minced
Salt
2 tbsp. chili powder

1/2 tsp. ground cumin seed
1/2 tsp. oregano leaves
1/2 tsp. pepper
1 bay leaf
1   15-oz. can red kidney beans
1 c. chopped sweet pickles
3 qt. boiling water
2 c. elbow macaroni

Brown the ground round in oil in a Dutch oven, stirring frequently. Add the tomatoes, tomato juice, onions, garlic, 4 teaspoons salt, chili powder, cumin, oregano and pepper and cover. Simmer for 1 hour. Drain the kidney beans and stir into tomato mixture. Stir in pickles and cook for 30 minutes longer. Remove the bay leaf. Add 1 tablespoon salt to the boiling water and add macaroni gradually so that water continues to boil. Cook, stirring occasionally, until tender and drain in a colander. Combine with chili and mix well. Serve in bowls. 10 servings.

Macaroni Chili (above)

CHILI CASSEROLE

2 tbsp. butter or margarine	2 1-lb. cans chili with beans
1 clove of garlic, minced	1 8-oz. package spaghetti
3/4 c. chopped onion	3 c. shredded Cheddar cheese
1 lb. ground beef	1 c. sour cream
1 1-lb. 3-oz. can tomatoes	1/4 c. grated Parmesan cheese

Melt the butter in a large skillet and brown the garlic, onion and ground beef. Drain off excess fat and add tomatoes and chili. Simmer for about 45 minutes. Cook spaghetti according to package directions and drain. Remove the skillet from heat and stir in Cheddar cheese until melted. Fold in sour cream. Add the spaghetti and mix well. Turn into 2-quart casserole and top with Parmesan cheese. Bake for 45 minutes at 350 degrees. 10-12 servings.

Mrs. R. W. Graney, Charlotte, North Carolina

MACARONI MEDLEY

1 onion, chopped	1 tsp. paprika
1 clove of garlic, minced (opt.)	1 tsp. Worcestershire sauce
1 green pepper, chopped	2/3 c. tomato soup
4 tbsp. shortening	2 c. cooked macaroni
1 lb. hamburger	1/2 c. grated cheese
1 1/2 tsp. salt	Buttered bread cubes
1/4 tsp. pepper	

Cook the onion, garlic and green pepper in shortening in a large skillet until golden brown. Add the hamburger and seasonings and cook, stirring, for 5 minutes. Add the soup and 1/2 cup water and stir well. Place half the macaroni in a baking dish and sprinkle with half the cheese. Add half the hamburger mixture and repeat layers. Place bread cubes over the top. Bake in 350-degree oven for 25 to 30 minutes or until browned.

Mrs. C. W. Herlong, Jr., Dinsmore, Florida

SPICY SPAGHETTI MEAT SAUCE

1 lb. hamburger	1 tsp. salt
1/4 c. chopped onions	1/4 tsp. pepper
1/4 c. chopped green pepper	2 tsp. Worcestershire sauce
1/4 c. olive oil	1 tsp. celery salt
2 cans tomato sauce	2 tsp. garlic salt
2 tomato sauce cans water	8 drops of hot sauce
2 cans tomato paste	2 tsp. chili powder
2 tsp. chopped parsley	1 can mushrooms

Brown the hamburger, onions and green pepper in olive oil in a large skillet, then add remaining ingredients. Simmer for at least 4 hours, adding water as needed and stirring occasionally. Serve over cooked spaghetti.

Mrs. Carroll Wood, Hugo, Oklahoma

PASTITSIO

1 lge. onion, chopped fine	Salt and pepper to taste
1/2 c. butter	1/2 c. white wine
2 lb. ground beef	1 lb. elbow macaroni
1/2 can tomato paste	1 lb. grated Parmesan cheese
1/2 c. water	2 eggs, well beaten
1/2 tsp. ground cinnamon	1 c. milk
1/2 tsp. ground nutmeg	

Saute the onion in half the butter. Add the ground beef and cook, stirring, until brown. Add the tomato paste and water and stir. Add the spices, seasonings and wine and simmer until thickened. Cook macaroni according to package directions and drain. Melt remaining butter and pour over macaroni, mixing carefully. Spread half the macaroni in a 9 x 13-inch baking pan and sprinkle with half the cheese. Pour beef sauce over cheese and cover with remaining macaroni. Top with remaining cheese. Mix the eggs and milk and pour over cheese. Bake at 350 degrees for 45 minutes. Cool slightly and cut in squares to serve. 12 servings.

Mrs. George Dowqwillo, Gunter AFB, Alabama

CASSEROLE FOR A CROWD

1 12-oz. package noodles	1 c. sour cream
1 1/2 lb. ground beef	1/4 c. chopped pimento
1 c. chopped onions	1/4 tsp. pepper
1 can whole kernel corn	1/2 tsp. salt
1 can cream of chicken soup	1 c. buttered crumbs
1 can cream of mushroom soup	

Cook the noodles according to package directions and drain. Brown the ground beef and onions in a skillet. Drain the corn and add to beef mixture. Add the noodles and remaining ingredients except crumbs and place in 2 1/2-quart casserole. Top with crumbs. Bake at 350 degrees for 30 minutes.

Nancy Vecera, Bellaire, Texas

TEXAS MATADOR

1 10-oz. package egg noodles	2 8-oz. cans tomato sauce
2 lb. ground beef	2 cloves of garlic, minced
3 tsp. salt	1 c. sour cream
3 tsp. sugar	1 3-oz. package cream cheese
1/2 tsp. pepper	6 green onions, chopped
1 16-oz. can tomatoes	1 c. grated cheese

Cook the noodles according to package directions and drain. Brown the ground beef with salt, sugar and pepper in a skillet. Add the tomatoes, tomato sauce and garlic and cook for 10 minutes over low heat. Add the noodles, sour cream, cream cheese and green onions. Place in a casserole and cover with grated cheese. Bake for 35 minutes at 350 degrees. 8 servings.

Mrs. A. C. Chamblee, Linden, Texas

Ripe Olive-Cabbage Loaf (below)

RIPE OLIVE-CABBAGE LOAF

1 med. head cabbage
1 gal. boiling water
Salt
1 1/2 c. pitted ripe olives
1 1/2 lb. lean ground beef
1/4 c. finely chopped onion
1 beaten egg
1/4 tsp. pepper

1/2 c. soft bread crumbs
1/4 c. milk
1/2 tsp. caraway seed
1/4 tsp. thyme
1 tbsp. flour
1 tbsp. melted butter
1 bouillon cube
1/3 c. white wine

Preheat oven to 350 degrees. Cut core from cabbage and pull leaves apart. Cook in boiling water with 2 tablespoons salt for about 10 minutes or until leaves are wilted, then drain. Reserve 1/4 cup olives for sauce and cut remaining olives in large pieces. Combine 1 3/4 teaspoons salt, olive pieces, beef, onion, egg, pepper, crumbs, milk, caraway seed and thyme and mix well. Line a greased loaf pan with cabbage leaves and cover with half the beef mixture, smoothing top. Arrange layer of cabbage leaves over beef mixture. Cover with remaining beef mixture, then top with cabbage. Cover with foil and place on a baking sheet. Bake for 1 hour and 15 minutes and remove foil. Drain the beef loaf and reserve liquid. Turn loaf out onto a heated platter and keep warm. Blend the flour with butter in a saucepan. Add enough water to reserved liquid to make 2/3 cup liquid and stir into flour mixture. Add the bouillon cube and wine and cook, stirring, until sauce boils and thickens slightly. Slice reserved olives and add to sauce. Serve with beef loaf. 6-8 servings.

OLIVE-STUFFED MEAT LOAF

1 1/2 c. crushed saltines
1/4 c. minced onions
1/2 c. sliced stuffed olives
2 eggs, slightly beaten

1 1/2 lb. lean ground beef
2 tbsp. grated horseradish
3/4 c. tomato juice

Preheat oven to 375 degrees. Combine crushed saltines, onions, olives, eggs, beef, horseradish and tomato juice in a bowl and mix well. Press into a greased 9 x 5-inch loaf pan. Arrange additional sliced olives on top. Bake for 1 hour and remove to a warm platter.

Mrs. E. B. Smith, Miami, Florida

DELUXE MEAT LOAF

2 med. stalks celery, chopped
1 med. onion, minced
1 med. carrot, minced
1 sm. can sliced mushrooms
1 med. green pepper, chopped
1/2 tsp. celery flakes
1/2 tsp. dry mustard
1/2 tsp. sage
1/2 tsp. salt

1/4 tsp. pepper
1/4 tsp. garlic salt
1 tbsp. soy sauce
1 tbsp. Worcestershire sauce
1 c. milk
2 eggs, beaten
1 c. oatmeal
1 lb. lean ground beef

Combine all ingredients except beef and mix well. Let stand for 30 minutes to 1 hour. Add the beef and mix thoroughly. Press into greased 8 x 5 x 3-inch loaf pan. Bake at 350 degrees for 1 hour and 15 minutes. May top with one 8-ounce can tomato sauce during last 15 minutes of baking, if desired.

Mrs. William M. Jarvis, Narrows, Virginia

SAGAS MEAT LOAF

1/2 c. molasses
1/4 c. vinegar
1/4 c. prepared mustard
1 c. tomato juice
2 eggs, beaten
3 c. soft bread crumbs

1 onion, finely chopped
1/2 c. chopped parsley
1 tbsp. salt
1 tsp. pepper
3 lb. ground beef

Combine 1/4 cup molasses, vinegar, mustard, tomato juice and eggs and mix well. Stir in the bread crumbs, onion, parsley, salt and pepper. Add the ground beef and mix well. Shape into a loaf. Place in a shallow baking dish and brush with 1 tablespoon molasses. Bake at 350 degrees for 1 hour and 30 minutes, brushing with remaining molasses occasionally.

Mrs. Leona Cashwell, Clinton, North Carolina

TEXAS BEEF LOAF

2 eggs, beaten
1/2 c. evaporated milk
1 sm. onion, chopped fine
1 tsp. salt

1 tbsp. Worcestershire sauce
1 1/2 c. crushed soda crackers
1/2 c. chopped celery
1 1/2 lb. ground chuck

Combine all ingredients and mix well. Pack in a baking dish. Bake at 350 degrees for 45 minutes. Let set for several minutes before slicing.

Mrs. M. R. Burnett, Grand Prairie, Texas

CALIFORNIA TAMALE LOAF

1 c. finely chopped celery	1 No. 2 can cream-style corn
1/2 c. finely chopped onion	2 well-beaten eggs
1 lge. green pepper, chopped	2 tsp. salt
4 tbsp. butter	1/2 tsp. pepper
1 lb. lean ground beef	1 tbsp. chili powder
2 cans tomato sauce	1 sm. can pitted ripe olives (opt.)
1 c. yellow cornmeal	

Cook the celery, onion and green pepper in butter in a saucepan until tender. Add the beef and cook until beef is light brown. Add the tomato sauce and mix well. Stir in cornmeal, corn, eggs, salt, pepper, chili powder and olives and mix well. Place in a greased loaf pan. Bake for 1 hour at 350 degrees.

Mrs. W. A. Winterrowd, Thorndale, Texas

MUSHROOM-STUFFED MEAT LOAF

2 6-oz. cans mushroom crowns	1/4 tsp. savory
1/4 c. margarine	1/4 c. minced parsley
1 tsp. lemon juice	2 eggs, well beaten
1 med. onion, minced	3 lb. ground chuck
4 c. bread crumbs	1/4 c. milk
1 tsp. salt	1/3 c. catsup
1/8 tsp. pepper	1 1/2 tsp. dry mustard
1/4 tsp. thyme	

Drain the mushrooms and slice, reserving 7 whole mushroom crowns. Cook the sliced mushrooms, margarine, lemon juice and onion in a skillet over medium heat for 3 minutes. Add the bread crumbs, salt, pepper, thyme, savory and parsley. Combine the eggs, ground chuck, milk, catsup and mustard and mix well. Pack half the ground chuck mixture in a 9 x 5 x 3-inch loaf pan. Spread the bread mixture over the ground chuck mixture and cover with remaining ground chuck mixture. Bake at 400 degrees for 1 hour and 10 minutes. Remove to heated platter and garnish with reserved mushroom crowns. 8 servings.

Mrs. Susan Lambdin, Montgomery, Alabama

BEEF LOAF AU GRATIN

1 egg	1 tbsp. Worcestershire sauce
1/2 c. milk	1/3 c. chopped onion
1 c. soft bread crumbs	1 lb. ground beef
1 tsp. salt	Sliced American cheese
1/4 tsp. pepper	Stuffed olives
1/2 tsp. dry mustard	

Combine all ingredients except the cheese and olives. Spread half the mixture in a loaf pan or casserole. Cover with cheese, then top with remaining beef mixture. Bake at 350 degrees for about 45 minutes and garnish with olives.

Mary Bernice Harper, Leggett, Texas

HOT LOAF

1 1/2 lb. ground beef
1/4 c. chopped onion
1 1/3 c. bread crumbs
2 tsp. salt
1 egg

4 tsp. horseradish
3/4 tsp. dry mustard
3 tbsp. catsup
1/2 c. milk

Combine all ingredients and blend well. Place in a loaf pan. Bake at 400 degrees for 1 hour.

Mrs. J. M. Teddlie, Beaumont, Texas

CRAZY MEAT LOAF

1 10-oz. package frozen mixed
   vegetables
1/4 c. butter or margarine
1 med. onion, chopped
2 c. soft bread crumbs
1/4 c. chopped parsley
1 1/4 tsp. salt

1/4 tsp. thyme
3/4 tsp. hot sauce
1 egg, slightly beaten
1/2 c. milk
1/2 tsp. basil
1 1/2 lb. ground beef
1 c. grated Cheddar cheese

Cook the mixed vegetables in boiling, salted water for 5 minutes and drain. Melt butter in a skillet. Add the onion and cook until tender but not brown. Add bread crumbs, parsley, 1/4 teaspoon salt, thyme and 1/4 teaspoon hot sauce. Combine the egg, milk, remaining salt, basil and remaining hot sauce in a mixing bowl. Add 1 cup bread crumb mixture and mix well. Add the ground chuck and mix well. Press 3/4 of the beef mixture over bottom and 3/4 up the sides of a 9 x 5 x 3-inch loaf pan, leaving center hollow. Combine remaining bread crumb mixture with mixed vegetables and cheese and turn into beef mixture in loaf pan. Cover with remaining beef mixture. Bake in 350-degree oven for 1 hour. Let stand for 10 minutes before turning out onto serving platter and serve with cheese sauce, if desired.

Crazy Meat Loaf (above)

Beef and Hash Brown Pie (below)

BEEF AND HASH BROWN PIE

1 egg, lightly beaten
3/4 c. soft bread crumbs
1/3 c. milk
2 tsp. salt
1/4 tsp. hickory smoke salt
1 tsp. monosodium glutamate
Pepper
1/2 c. minced onion
1/4 c. minced parsley
1 1/2 lb. lean ground beef

1 12-oz. package frozen hash
   brown potatoes, thawed
2 tbsp. melted butter
3/4 c. grated Cheddar cheese
1 8-oz. can tomato sauce
1/2 tsp. chili powder
1/2 tsp. prepared mustard
1/4 tsp. Worcestershire sauce
Dash of hot sauce

Combine the egg with bread crumbs, milk, 1 1/4 teaspoons salt, smoke salt, monosodium glutamate. 1/8 teaspoon pepper, onion and parsley and mix well. Add the beef and mix well. Spread on bottom and side of greased 9-inch pie plate. Mix the potatoes with remaining salt and dash of pepper. Spoon into beef shell and drizzle with butter. Bake at 350 degrees for 30 minutes or until beef mixture is browned. Sprinkle the cheese over potatoes and broil until cheese is melted and browned. Let stand for 5 minutes before cutting. Combine remaining ingredients in a saucepan and bring to a boil, stirring frequently. Serve with beef pie. 6-8 servings.

HOBOS

1 lb. hamburger
4 Irish potatoes, quartered
4 carrots

Catsup
4 onion slices

Shape the hamburger into 4 patties and place each patty on a square of aluminum foil. Place 1 potato and 1 carrot around each patty and spread catsup over patties. Place 1 onion slice on each patty. Fold the foil over and seal ends. Place on a baking sheet. Bake for 30 to 45 minutes at 350 degrees.

Melinda Marion, Dobson, North Carolina

BEEF-POTATO TOWERS

6 med. baked potatoes	1/2 tsp. pepper
1 lb. ground beef	2 eggs, beaten
1/2 c. chopped onion	4 tbsp. catsup
1 stalk celery, chopped	2 slices mild cheese
1 tsp. salt	Dried parsley flakes

Cut the potatoes in half. Scoop out pulp with spoon, place in a bowl and mash. Add the ground beef, onion, celery, salt, pepper, eggs and catsup and mix well. Fill the potato shells with the beef mixture and place in a shallow baking pan. Bake at 400 degrees for 30 to 35 minutes. Cut the cheese in narrow strips and place on potato mixture in crisscross fashion. Sprinkle with parsley and bake until the cheese is lightly browned.

Mrs. Linda Everhart, High Point, North Carolina

CABBAGE ROLL

10 lge. cabbage leaves	1 can tomatoes, well drained
1 lb. ground beef	1 lge. onion, chopped fine
1 c. bread crumbs	1 tsp. salt
Dash of cinnamon (opt.)	

Cook the cabbage leaves in a saucepan in enough water to cover for 2 minutes. Drain and set aside. Mix remaining ingredients. Place on cabbage leaves, roll and secure with toothpicks. Wrap rolls in foil and place in a baking pan. Bake at 300 degrees for 40 minutes. 4-6 servings.

Mrs. C. G. Buckler, Comanche, Texas

GARDEN CASSEROLE

1 c. sliced onions	3/4 tsp. salt
1 lb. ground beef	1/8 tsp. pepper
3 tbsp. fat	1 tbsp. brown sugar
1 green pepper, chopped	3 c. seasoned mashed potatoes
1 c. chopped celery	2 tbsp. melted butter
1 c. diced carrots	Parsley sprigs
4 lge. firm tomatoes, quartered	

Brown the onions and beef in fat in a skillet, stirring constantly. Add the green pepper, celery, carrots, tomatoes, seasonings and sugar and simmer for 20 minutes. Pour into a 2-quart casserole and top with potatoes. Brush with butter. Bake at 350 degrees until golden brown and garnish with parsley.

Twila Champlin, Loranger, Louisiana

Italian Biscuit Roll-Ups (below)

ITALIAN BISCUIT ROLL-UPS

1 lb. ground beef, crumbled	1 tsp. salt
1 1 1/2-oz. package spaghetti	1/4 c. shortening
sauce mix	1/4 c. chopped onion
1 8-oz. can tomato sauce	1/2 to 3/4 c. milk
2 c. sifted flour	1 c. water
1 tbsp. baking powder	1 c. shredded sharp Cheddar cheese

Cook the ground beef in a skillet until brown, stirring frequently, then stir in spaghetti sauce mix and tomato sauce. Simmer for about 10 minutes or until thickened. Sift the flour, baking powder and salt together into a bowl and cut in shortening until mixture resembles coarse crumbs. Stir in onion and blend in enough milk to make a soft dough. Turn out onto lightly floured board or pastry cloth and knead gently for 30 seconds. Roll out to a 12 x 16-inch rectangle. Spread 1 cup beef mixture evenly over dough and roll as for jelly roll, starting at narrow edge. Seal edges securely and cut into 1-inch thick slices. Place on lightly greased baking sheet. Bake in 425-degree oven for 12 to 15 minutes or until golden brown. Blend the water into remaining beef mixture and heat through. Spoon beef sauce over Biscuit Roll-Ups and sprinkle cheese over beef sauce. 6 servings.

CALCUTTA BEEF

3 tbsp. butter	1 1/2 tbsp. curry powder
2 onions, sliced	1 tbsp. flour
1 1/2 lb. ground beef	2 c. chicken stock
1 tsp. salt	1/2 can peas
1 c. tomatoes	Cooked rice
1 tart apple, chopped	Raisins
1 tbsp. chopped green pepper	1 box shredded coconut

Melt the butter in a skillet. Add onions, beef and salt and cook until brown. Add the tomatoes, apple and green pepper. Mix the curry powder with flour and stir in the chicken stock until smooth. Stir into the beef mixture. Cook for several minutes and place in casserole. Bake at 350 degrees for 30 minutes. Place peas on top and bake for 5 minutes longer. Serve on rice. Serve raisins and coconut browned in additional butter in side dishes.

Mrs. M. L. Ballew, Vicksburg, Mississippi

SKILLET BEEF

2 lb. hamburger	1 can chili beans
1/2 lb. cheese, grated	1 c. hominy
1 c. crushed corn chips	

Cook the hamburger in a heavy skillet until partially done, stirring frequently. Add the cheese and mix well. Cook till hamburger is well done. Add the corn chips and stir in beans and hominy. Heat through.

Mrs. N. J. Dedear, Round Rock, Texas

CHILI BEANS ON HAMBURGER BUN

1 lb. ground beef	1 c. canned tomatoes
1 tbsp. shortening	1 c. cooked kidney beans
1/2 c. diced green pepper	1/8 tsp. pepper
1/4 c. minced onion	2 tsp. chili powder
1 1/2 tsp. salt	

Brown the ground beef in shortening in a large skillet or Dutch oven. Add the green pepper, onion, salt and tomatoes. Cook, stirring occasionally, for about 10 minutes or until thickened. Add the beans, pepper and chili powder and cook over low heat for 5 to 6 minutes. 8 servings.

Rachel Young, Lavaca, Arkansas

HAMBURGER STROGANOFF

1/2 c. finely chopped onion	1 tsp. pepper
1/4 c. butter	1 c. sliced mushrooms
1 lb. ground beef	1 c. cream of chicken soup
2 tbsp. flour	1 c. sour cream
1 tsp. salt	

Cook the onion in butter in a saucepan over medium heat until transparent. Add the beef and cook, stirring, until beef is light brown. Add the flour, salt, pepper, mushrooms and soup and cook for 5 minutes. Add the sour cream and simmer for 15 minutes longer. Serve over rice and garnish with paprika.

Delane Dees, Evergreen, Alabama

Braised Short Ribs of Beef with Celery (below)

BRAISED SHORT RIBS OF BEEF WITH CELERY

3 lb. short ribs of beef	6 med. white onions
4 tbsp. all-purpose flour	5 stalks celery
3 tsp. salt	1/2 tsp. pepper
2 tbsp. shortening	1/2 tsp. thyme leaves
2 c. boiling water	

Trim excess fat from the ribs and discard. Cut ribs into 3-inch pieces. Mix 3 tablespoons flour with salt and dredge ribs with the seasoned flour. Brown on all sides in shortening in a deep skillet. Add the boiling water and cover skillet. Simmer for 2 hours or until beef is almost tender. Add the onions and cover. Cook for 10 minutes. Cut the celery into 2-inch pieces. Add celery, pepper and thyme to beef mixture and cover. Cook for about 25 minutes longer or until the vegetables are tender. Remove beef and vegetables to a heated platter. Blend remaining flour with 2 tablespoons cold water and stir into liquid in skillet. Cook for 1 minute and serve with beef mixture. 6-8 servings.

SHORT RIBS WITH PARSLEY DUMPLINGS

2 lb. short ribs	4 carrots, sliced
1 1/2 c. flour	2 onions, sliced
Salt	2 potatoes, cubed
1/4 tsp. pepper	2 tsp. baking powder
1 stick margarine	2 tbsp. chopped parsley
1 1-lb. can tomatoes	2 tbsp. salad oil
2 cloves of garlic, minced	1/2 c. milk
1 tbsp. Worcestershire sauce	

Cut the ribs into serving pieces. Combine 1/2 cup flour, 1 tablespoon salt and pepper. Dredge ribs with the flour mixture and brown in margarine in a kettle. Add the tomatoes, garlic and Worcestershire sauce and cover. Simmer for 1 hour and 30 minutes. Add the carrots, onions and potatoes and simmer for 45 minutes longer. Mix remaining flour, baking powder, 1 teaspoon salt and parsley. Add the oil and milk and stir until mixed. Add 2 cups water to the ribs mixture and bring to a boil. Drop flour mixture by tablespoonfuls into rib mixture. Reduce heat and simmer for 15 minutes. 5 servings.

Mrs. Anna Canalle, Winchester, Virginia

BRAISED SHORT RIBS

8 beef short ribs	8 sm. potatoes
3 tsp. salt	8 carrots
3/4 tsp. pepper	8 sm. onions
2 tbsp. salad oil	2 tbsp. flour

Season the ribs with salt and pepper and brown over high heat on all sides in oil in a heavy iron skillet. Add 2 cups boiling water and cover tightly. Simmer for 1 hour. Add the vegetables and cook for 1 hour or until beef is tender. Remove ribs and vegetables to a platter. Mix flour and 3 tablespoons water and stir into liquid in skillet. Cook until thickened. 6-8 servings.

BEEF SHORT RIBS WITH RAISIN SAUCE

3 lb. beef short ribs	1 tbsp. flour
Salt and pepper to taste	2 tbsp. vinegar
3 tbsp. fat	2 tbsp. lemon juice
1 onion, chopped	1/4 tsp. grated lemon rind
1/2 c. (firmly packed) brown sugar	1 bay leaf
1 tsp. dry mustard	1 1/2 c. water
1/2 c. raisins	

Cut the ribs into serving pieces and season with salt and pepper. Brown in hot fat in a heavy skillet. Drain off excess fat, add the onion and cook until onion is tender. Combine remaining ingredients in a saucepan and bring to a boil. Pour over the ribs and cover tightly. Cook over low heat for about 2 hours or until ribs are tender. Sauce may be thickened with additional flour, if desired. 6-8 servings.

Mrs. Dent Lamar, Selma, Alabama

SPICED BEEF SHORT RIBS

3 lb. beef short ribs	1 c. dried apricots
1 1/2 tsp. salt	1/2 c. sugar
1/4 c. flour	1/2 tsp. allspice
2 tbsp. shortening or drippings	1/4 tsp. ground cloves
1 1/4 c. water	1/2 tsp. cinnamon
1 c. prunes	3 tbsp. vinegar

Cut the ribs into serving pieces and season with salt. Dredge with flour and brown in shortening in a skillet. Add the water and cover. Simmer for 1 hour. Add prunes, apricots and remaining ingredients and simmer for 1 hour or until beef is tender. Thicken the liquid for gravy, if desired. 6 servings.

Mrs. Edgar George, Michie, Tennessee

SWEET-SOUR SHORT RIBS

3 lb. short ribs	1/4 c. white vinegar
1/4 c. bacon drippings	1 c. unsweetened pineapple juice
2 tbsp. brown sugar	1 tbsp. soy sauce
2 tbsp. flour	1 c. diced onion
1 tsp. salt	1 c. diced green pepper
1/4 c. water	1 c. pineapple chunks

Cut the ribs into serving pieces and brown in bacon drippings in a skillet. Cover skillet. Bake at 375 degrees until beef is tender and pour off excess fat. Mix the sugar, flour and salt with water in a saucepan until smooth. Add the vinegar, pineapple juice and soy sauce and cook until slightly thickened. Add the onion, green pepper and pineapple and pour over the ribs. Cover and bake for 15 minutes longer. 6-8 servings.

Mrs. George Harrison, Huntington, West Virginia

MANZO STRACOTTO

1 1/4 lb. beef chuck	with mushrooms
1 tsp. salt	1 c. water
1/8 tsp. pepper	8 sm. white onions
2 tbsp. flour	8 sm. scraped carrots
2 tbsp. shortening	3 peeled potatoes
1 15 1/2-oz. can spaghetti sauce	

Cut the beef into 1-inch pieces. Mix the salt, pepper and flour and dredge beef with seasoned flour. Melt the shortening in a skillet. Add the beef and brown well on all sides. Add spaghetti sauce and water and bring to a boil. Cover and reduce heat. Simmer for about 1 hour and 30 minutes. Add the onions, carrots and potatoes and simmer for about 45 minutes longer or until vegetables are tender. 4 servings.

Manzo Stracotto (above)

BEEF BALL SOUP

1 1/2 lb. lean ground beef	1 lge. onion, minced
1 med. bell pepper, minced	1 c. frozen green peas
1 egg	2 tbsp. sugar
1 1/2 tsp. salt	1/2 tsp. pepper
2/3 c. corn flake crumbs	2 c. water
4 med. carrots, sliced	2 No. 303 cans tomatoes
4 med. potatoes, quartered	

Combine the ground beef, bell pepper, egg, 1/2 teaspoon salt and corn flake crumbs in a large bowl and mix thoroughly. Shape into 1-inch balls. Place the vegetables in a 4-quart kettle and sprinkle with remaining salt, sugar and pepper. Place meatballs over vegetables and pour water and tomatoes over meatballs. Bring to a boil and reduce heat. Simmer for 1 hour and 15 minutes. 6 servings.

Mrs. R. P. Welch, Jonesboro, Arkansas

HEARTY FRESH VEGETABLE SOUP

1 4-lb. beef soup bone with meat	2 stalks celery with leaves
2 qt. cold water	2 carrots, quartered
2 tbsp. salt	4 c. diced potatoes
6 peppercorns	1 1/2 c. sliced carrots
2 med. onions, quartered	2/3 c. sliced celery
2 sprigs of parsley	1 c. snap beans, cut in pieces
	6 c. canned tomatoes

Combine first 8 ingredients in a kettle and cover. Simmer for 2 hours. Remove soup bone, trim off meat and set aside. Strain the stock and pour into kettle. Add remaining ingredients and cover. Cook until vegetables are tender. Add the meat and heat through. 10-12 servings.

Josie Leal, Seadrift, Texas

SAVORY STEW

2 lb. beef chuck	1/2 tsp. pepper
2 tbsp. fat	1/2 tsp. paprika
4 c. boiling water	Dash of allspice or cloves
1 tsp. lemon juice	1 tsp. sugar
1 tsp. Worcestershire sauce	6 carrots, diced
1 clove of garlic (opt.)	1 lb. small onions
2 bay leaves	2 c. diced potatoes
1 tbsp. salt	

Cut the beef chuck in 1 1/2-inch cubes and brown in fat in a large saucepan. Add the boiling water, lemon juice, Worcestershire sauce, garlic, bay leaves, salt, pepper, paprika, allspice and sugar and simmer for 2 hours. Add the carrots, onions and potatoes and cook until the vegetables are done.

Mrs. S. C. Ray, Austin, Texas

Ripe Olive-Beef Stroganoff (below)

RIPE OLIVE-BEEF STROGANOFF

1 2-lb. flank steak	2 beef bouillon cubes
2 onions, sliced	1/4 tsp. nutmeg
1/4 c. oil	1 c. pitted ripe olives
1 1/2 tsp. salt	1 tbsp. cornstarch
1/4 tsp. pepper	1 c. sour cream

Cut the steak diagonally into 1/8-inch thick strips. Brown the steak and onions in hot oil in a skillet, then add the salt, pepper, 1/2 cup water, bouillon cubes and nutmeg. Cover the skillet. Simmer for 10 minutes. Cut the olives into chunks. Mix the cornstarch with 2 tablespoons water and stir into the steak mixture. Cook, stirring constantly, until thickened. Stir in the olives and sour cream and heat through, but do not boil. Serve with rice. 6 servings.

KABOBS

1 tbsp. lemon juice	Celery chunks
3 tbsp. salad oil	Green pepper chunks
1 clove of garlic, crushed	Pineapple cubes
1/4 tsp. salt	Mushroom caps
1 tsp. water	Unpeeled apple slices
Dash of pepper	1/4 c. honey
Dash of monosodium glutamate	1/4 c. pineapple juice
3 lb. shank beef, cut in cubes	1/4 tsp. ginger
Carrot chunks	

Combine the lemon juice, oil, garlic, salt, water, pepper and monosodium glutamate and mix well. Add the beef and marinate for 2 hours. Drain beef and reserve marinade. Cook the carrots, celery and green pepper chunks in water until partially done, then drain. Place the beef, pineapple, mushrooms, apple slices and carrot, celery and green pepper chunks on skewers. Place on broiler pan. Combine remaining ingredients with reserved marinade and brush on kabobs. Broil 4 inches from heat for 15 to 20 minutes, basting with sauce and turning frequently. Serve over rice, if desired. 4 servings.

Barbara Schilde, Hahnville, Louisiana

BEEF AND BEANS SKILLET DINNER

1/2 lb. stew beef	1 c. chopped celery
2 tbsp. oil	1 tbsp. cornstarch
1 med. onion, chopped	1 tbsp. soy sauce
2 No. 303 cans green beans	1 sm. can button mushrooms

Brown the beef in oil in a skillet. Add the onion, beans and celery and cook for 4 to 6 minutes, stirring frequently. Mix the cornstarch and soy sauce. Drain the mushrooms and add enough water to the mushroom liquid to make 3/4 cup liquid. Stir into the cornstarch mixture. Add to the beef mixture, stirring constantly, then add the mushrooms. Cover the skillet. Cook over medium heat for about 1 hour or until beef is tender. 6 servings.

Mrs. Anne Plummer, Birmingham, Alabama

SAFFRONED BEEF AND BEANS

1 c. dry navy beans	1/8 tsp. pepper
2 tsp. salt	1/4 tsp. crumbled saffron
2 tbsp. salad oil	1 tsp. brown sugar
1 lb. beef, cut in cubes	1/2 c. dry white wine
3 ripe tomatoes, quartered	1 No. 2 can whole kernel corn
1 med. onion, thinly sliced	1 med. green pepper, thinly sliced

Rinse the beans thoroughly and place in a large saucepan with enough water to cover. Bring to a boil and reduce heat. Simmer for 2 hours. Add 1 teaspoon salt and simmer for 1 hour longer or until beans are tender, adding water as needed to keep beans covered. Heat the oil in a large, heavy skillet. Add the beef and brown over high heat. Add the tomatoes, onion, remaining salt, pepper, saffron, brown sugar and wine and simmer until beef is tender. Drain the beans, then add the corn, green pepper and beans to the beef mixture. Cook until green pepper is tender. 4 servings.

Mrs. Remington McConnell, Atlanta, Georgia

BEEF IN WINE

3 lb. lean stew beef	3/4 c. red wine
1 can cream of mushroom soup	1/4 c. brandy
1 can onion soup	

Preheat oven to 350 degrees. Place all ingredients except brandy in a 3-quart casserole and cover tightly. Bake for 3 hours and 30 minutes. Stir in brandy and cover. Bake for 20 to 30 minutes longer and serve over rice. 6 servings.

Mrs. A. F. Jordan, Alexandria, Virginia

Holiday Beef in Wine Sauce (below)

HOLIDAY BEEF IN WINE SAUCE

1 to 2 lb. boneless sirloin steak	1/4 c. port
2 tbsp. oil	2 tbsp. orange marmalade
1 3/4-oz. envelope mushroom	1 1-lb. can whole onions
gravy mix	Cooked rice or wild rice
3/4 c. water	

Cut the steak in strips and brown in oil in a large skillet. Blend in the gravy mix, then stir in the water, port, marmalade and onions. Cook over medium heat for 10 minutes. Serve on rice. 6-8 servings.

CURRIED BEEF PAPRIKA

4 lb. beef shoulder	1/4 tsp. paprika
1/2 c. butter or margarine	1 10 1/2-oz. can beef broth
2 tsp. salt	2 c. sour cream
1 tbsp. sugar	2/3 c. all-purpose flour
4 tsp. curry powder	2/3 c. cold water
1 1/4 tsp. pepper	1 8-oz. package broad noodles

Cut the beef into 1 1/2-inch cubes and brown in butter in a Dutch oven. Sprinkle with salt, sugar, curry powder, pepper, and paprika and stir in the broth and sour cream. Mix the flour with water and stir into beef mixture. Cover the Dutch oven. Simmer for 1 hour or until beef is tender, stirring occasionally. Cook the noodles according to package directions. Serve the beef mixture over noodles. 8 servings.

Mrs. Wilmer E. Harper, Lucedale, Mississippi

POLYNESIAN STEAK

1 lb. steak, cut in 2-in. cubes	2 tbsp. honey or syrup
1 c. water	2 tbsp. cooking sherry or sauterne
2 lge. onions, sliced thin	2 cloves of garlic, minced
2 tbsp. soy sauce	1/2 tsp. salt

Place the steak in a shallow baking dish. Mix remaining ingredients and pour over the steak. Marinate for 3 hours, stirring frequently. Place baking dish under broiler. Broil until steak is done, stirring frequently and serve with rice. 2 servings.

Mrs. Arnold Pierson, Johnson, Tennessee

SUKIYAKI

2 1/2 lb. prime sirloin	1 c. finely chopped onions
1 8-oz. can bamboo shoots	1 tbsp. sugar
1 8 1/2-oz. can water chestnuts	1/4 c. soy sauce
2 c. thinly sliced carrots	1 c. beef broth
2 c. thinly sliced celery	1 tbsp. angostura aromatic bitters

Cut the fat from outer edge of sirloin and reserve. Freeze the sirloin until hard, then cut into 1 1/2-inch paper-thin strips. Drain the bamboo shoots and water chestnuts and slice. Mix with the carrots, celery and onions. Combine remaining ingredients in a bowl. Dice the reserved fat and fry in a large skillet until crisp. Remove crisp pieces and add the sirloin to hot fat. Cook over high heat until browned. Add the celery mixture and stir well. Add the broth mixture and cover. Simmer for 5 minutes or until vegetables are tender-crisp. 6 servings.

Sukiyaki (above)

BEEF SUPREME

1 med. onion, chopped
2 tbsp. butter
2 lb. round steak, cut in cubes
1/4 c. flour
1 can mushroom soup
1 can cream of celery soup

3/4 tsp. salt
1/4 tsp. pepper
1 tbsp. Worcestershire sauce
6 med. potatoes, diced
3 med. carrots, diced

Saute the onion in butter in a skillet until tender. Dredge the steak with flour. Add to onion and cook until brown. Stir in the soups, salt, pepper and Worcestershire sauce and cover. Cook over low heat until steak is tender. Add the potatoes and carrots and cook until carrots are tender. 6-8 servings.

Betty Anne Hayes, Willacoochee, Georgia

CHINESE RICE CASSEROLE

1 1/2 to 2 lb. round steak
1 tbsp. oil
2 pimentos
1 can sliced mushrooms
3/4 c. sliced celery
3/4 c. diced onion
1/2 c. chopped green pepper

1/2 c. rice
1 tbsp. soy sauce
1/4 tsp. instant minced garlic
1 can cream of mushroom soup
1 c. water
Salt and pepper to taste

Cut the steak into small cubes and brown in oil in a skillet. Drain the pimentos and mushrooms and chop the pimentos. Add pimentos and mushrooms to the steak. Add remaining ingredients and mix well. Cover skillet. Bake at 325 degrees for 1 hour and 30 minutes. 6 servings.

Mrs. Gilbert G. Leonard, Quantico, Virginia

BEEF IN SAVORY SAUCE

3 tbsp. flour
1/2 tsp. salt
Dash of pepper
1/2 tsp. monosodium glutamate
1 lb. lean beef
2 tbsp. butter

1   10 3/4-oz. can beef gravy
2 tbsp. orange juice
2 tbsp. currant jelly
1   3 1/2-oz. can broiled mushrooms
2 tbsp. sliced stuffed olives
1 bay leaf

Mix the flour, salt, pepper and monosodium glutamate. Cut the beef into 1-inch cubes and dredge with the flour mixture. Brown in the butter in a Dutch oven over medium heat. Add the gravy, orange juice and currant jelly and stir until mixed. Bring to a boil and stir in sliced mushrooms, olives and bay leaf. Reduce heat and cover. Simmer for 1 hour and 30 minutes or until beef is tender, stirring frequently and adding water, if needed. Remove the bay leaf and serve with rice.

Mrs. Myrtle Miller Garth, Florence, Alabama

ROLL FLEISCH

1 thin round steak	1/2 c. chopped bacon
Salt and pepper to taste	Flour
1/2 c. chopped onions	

Trim the steak and sprinkle with salt and pepper. Mix the onions and bacon and spread on the steak. Roll as for jelly roll and tie with string or secure with toothpicks. Flour lightly and brown in small amount of fat in heavy saucepan. Add 1/4 cup water and cover tightly. Simmer for 1 hour and 30 minutes to 2 hours, adding water, if needed.

Mrs. Roland Ludtke, Austin, Texas

STEW WITH RAVIOLI DUMPLINGS

2 lb. boneless beef chuck	1 c. spaghetti sauce with mushrooms
3 tbsp. flour	1/8 tsp. basil
1 tsp. salt	8 sm. white onions
3 tbsp. oil	1 10-oz. box frozen peas
1 c. beef bouillon	1 15 1/2-oz. can beef ravioli

Cut the beef into 1 1/2-inch cubes. Mix the flour and 1/2 teaspoon salt and dredge beef with seasoned flour. Heat the oil in a saucepan. Add beef and brown well on all sides. Add the bouillon, spaghetti sauce and remaining salt and cover. Cook over low heat for about 50 minutes. Add the onions and simmer for 25 minutes. Break frozen peas into pieces, add to beef mixture and cover. Cook for 10 minutes longer. Spoon beef ravioli on top and cover. Heat for 5 minutes. 4-6 servings.

Stew with Ravioli Dumplings (above)

51

FAVORITE BEEF STROGANOFF

1 1/2 lb. sirloin steak	1 clove of garlic, crushed
Flour	6 tbsp. butter
1 1/2 tsp. salt	1 10 1/2-oz. can consomme
1/2 tsp. pepper	1 pt. sour cream
2 onions, finely chopped	1 tsp. paprika
1/2 lb. mushrooms, chopped	1 tbsp. Worcestershire sauce

Cut the steak into strips and dredge with flour. Season with 1 teaspoon salt and 1/4 teaspoon pepper. Saute the onions, mushrooms and garlic in butter in a skillet for 5 minutes. Add the steak and cook over high heat for 3 minutes, stirring constantly. Remove steak and vegetables from skillet. Blend 2 tablespoons flour into 2 tablespoons drippings in the skillet. Add the consomme and cook, stirring, until smooth and thickened. Stir in the sour cream and remaining salt and pepper and place over low heat. Add the paprika, Worcestershire sauce, beef and vegetables and heat through. 4 servings.

Mrs. Kenneth F. Harper, South Fort Mitchell, Kentucky

BEEF TAJINE

1 lge. onion, chopped	2 lb. beef, cut in cubes
1/2 c. chopped parsley	4 c. green peas
1 tsp. paprika	Salt and pepper to taste
4 tbsp. oil	Flour
1 bay leaf	

Saute the onion, parsley and paprika in oil for 5 minutes, then add the bay leaf, beef and enough water to cover. Simmer until beef is tender and remove bay leaf. Add the peas, salt and pepper and cover tightly. Cook for 20 minutes, adding water, if needed. Thicken to desired consistency with flour mixed with small amount of water. 4-6 servings.

Evelyn Watson, Milton, Florida

SOUR BEEF

1 lge. onion, sliced	3/4 c. vinegar
6 peppercorns	1 c. water
2 bay leaves	1 3-lb. pot roast
1 tsp. salt	2 tbsp. butter

Combine first 6 ingredients in a glass mixing bowl. Add the roast and refrigerate for 1 to 3 days. Drain roast. Remove onion from marinade and reserve. Strain and reserve marinade. Melt the butter in a Dutch oven. Add the roast and brown on all sides. Add reserved onion and 1/2 cup reserved marinade. Simmer for 1 hour and 30 minutes to 2 hours, adding remaining marinade as needed. Thicken the gravy, if desired. Serve beef and gravy with potato dumplings or mashed potatoes.

Mrs. Warner Jackson, Stuart, Florida

CARNE QUISADA

2 lb. round steak, cut in cubes	3 tbsp. minced onion
2 tbsp. shortening	1 lge. can tomatoes
Salt to taste	Flour
1/2 tsp. pepper	1 6-oz. can tomato sauce
4 cloves of garlic, mashed	

Brown the steak in shortening in a 10-inch skillet. Add the salt, pepper, garlic, onion and tomatoes and cook, stirring frequently, until liquid has evaporated. Add the tomato sauce and 2 cups water and bring to a boil. Mix 1/4 cup flour with 1/4 cup water and stir into the steak mixture. Cook for about 30 minutes. 6-8 servings.

Bertha E. Perez, Pharr, Texas

BEEF AND TANGY APPLESAUCE

1 6 to 8-lb. standing rib of beef	4 tsp. prepared horseradish
1 1-lb. can applesauce	4 tbsp. sour cream

Let beef stand at room temperature for 1 hour. Place, fat side up, on rack in a shallow pan and insert meat thermometer so tip will be in center. Roast at 325 degrees for 22 minutes per pound or 140 degrees on meat thermometer for medium rare or to desired degree of doneness. Let roast stand for 20 minutes in a warm place before carving, as roast will continue to cook after being removed from oven. Cut across the grain into thin slices. Blend remaining ingredients in a bowl and serve with beef.

Beef and Tangy Applesauce (above)

DEVILED POT ROAST

1 4 to 5-lb. boneless beef roast (chuck, shoulder, or rump)	5 tbsp. salad oil, divided
About 1/2 c. small stuffed olives	1 lge. onion, chopped
Salt and pepper	1/8 tsp. thyme (opt.)
All-purpose flour	1/8 tsp. marjoram (opt.)
	1 1-lb. can tomatoes, undrained

Cut slits about 1 1/2 inches deep in roast and into each of these push an olive. Season roast with salt and pepper; dredge with flour. Heat 3 tablespoons oil in heavy skillet and brown meat thoroughly on all sides. Saute onion in 2 tablespoons oil in Dutch oven large enough to accommodate the roast. Transfer browned roast to Dutch oven; sprinkle with additional salt, pepper, thyme, and marjoram. Spoon tomatoes slowly over roast so as not to disturb seasonings; cover tightly. Bake at 300 degrees about 3 1/2 hours or until meat is quite tender. Baste the roast occasionally. When meat is done, remove from pot and chill gravy thoroughly so fat may be skimmed from top. Reheat whole or sliced roast in the gravy. Good served hot or cold. 4-6 servings.

POT ROAST WITH TOMATO GRAVY

1 4 to 5-lb. beef blade pot roast	Salt and pepper to taste
4 tbsp. fat	1 No. 303 can tomatoes
1 clove of garlic (opt.)	4 tbsp. flour
1/2 tsp. thyme	Cooked noodles
1/2 c. vinegar	

Brown the pot roast in fat in a Dutch oven. Add the garlic, thyme, vinegar, salt, pepper and 1/3 cup water and cover. Cook over low heat for 2 hours. Add tomatoes and simmer for about 1 hour longer or until roast is tender. Remove roast to hot platter. Remove garlic and discard. Mix the flour with 1/4 cup water and stir into tomato mixture. Cook until thick, stirring constantly and pour over noodles. Serve with roast.

Mrs. A. J. Wolfson, Brandywine, Maryland

POPPY SEED POT ROAST WITH SOUR CREAM GRAVY

1 tsp. salad oil	1 lb. carrots, cut into pieces
1 5-lb. beef pot roast	1 can peas, drained
2 c. water	Flour
2 1/2 tsp. salt	1 tsp. paprika
1/4 tsp. pepper	1/2 c. sour cream
2 tsp. poppy seed	

Heat the oil in a heavy kettle and brown the roast well on all sides. Add the water, 1 1/2 teaspoons salt, pepper and poppy seed and cover kettle. Simmer for 3 hours and 30 minutes and remove the roast from kettle. Place the carrots in a saucepan. Drain enough of the broth from the kettle to cover carrots and bring to a boil. Simmer until carrots are done and pour back into the kettle. Add the peas and heat liquid to boiling point. Thicken with flour mixed with water and season with remaining salt and paprika. Remove from heat, add sour cream and mix well. Serve with pot roast.

Mrs. Pearl W. Williams, Winder, Georgia

MAN'S BOAST — THE ROAST

1 4 to 6-lb. rolled cross ribs of beef	Salt and pepper to taste

Season the beef with salt and pepper and place, fat side up, on rack in a shallow baking pan. Roast at 325 degrees for about 2 hours for rare or to desired doneness. Let stand for 20 minutes in warm place before carving, as roast will continue to cook after being removed from oven. 12 servings.

Man's Boast — The Roast (above)

MARINATED BEEF ROAST

2/3 c. tarragon vinegar	1/2 tsp. prepared mustard
1/2 c. light corn syrup	1/4 tsp. pepper
1/4 c. corn oil	2 lb. sliced cooked beef
2 tbsp. Worcestershire sauce	2 onions, thinly sliced
1 tsp. salt	

Combine the first 7 ingredients for marinade. Place the beef and onions in a shallow dish, pour the marinade over the beef and refrigerate for at least 3 hours. Remove the beef and onions from marinade and serve cold. 8 servings.

Mrs. J. P. La Groon, McCormick, South Carolina

HUNGARIAN POT ROAST

1 4-lb. chuck or rump roast	1 4-oz. can sliced mushrooms
1 tbsp. paprika	4 lge. onions, quartered
2 tsp. salt	8 sm. carrots
1/4 tsp. pepper	2 8-oz. cans tomato sauce
2 tbsp. oil	2 tbsp. minced parsley
1/2 c. water	1 c. sour cream (opt.)
1 bay leaf	

Trim excess fat from the roast. Sprinkle the roast with paprika, salt and pepper and brown in hot oil in Dutch oven. Add the water and bay leaf and cover. Simmer for 1 hour and 30 minutes to 2 hours or until the roast is tender. Drain the mushrooms and add to Dutch oven. Add the onions, carrots and tomato sauce and cover. Simmer for 60 minutes or until vegetables are done. Add parsley and remove from heat. Stir in the sour cream slowly and serve with cooked noodles. 6-8 servings.

Mrs. W. H. Chasteen, Morrill, Kentucky

ELEGANT BEEF WELLINGTON

1 4 to 4 1/2-lb. beef filet	Duxelles
Salt and pepper to taste	1 egg
Butter Pastry	Sesame seed

Place beef on rack in a shallow baking pan and sprinkle with salt and pepper. Roast at 425 degrees for 30 minutes. Let stand until cool, then trim off all fat. Roll Butter Pastry on a floured surface to rectangle about 3 inches longer than roast and 12 to 13 inches wide. Press Duxelles into pastry, leaving an inch uncovered on all edges. Place beef on pastry. Moisten pastry edges and enclose beef, pressing edges together firmly. Trim off excess pastry from ends so single layer covers ends of roast. Place roll, seam side down, in a shallow baking pan. Cut decorations from pastry trimmings and place on top. Brush pastry with egg beaten with 1 tablespoon water and sprinkle with sesame seed. Bake at 400 degrees for 30 to 35 minutes or until browned. Let stand for 15 to 20 minutes before slicing.

Butter Pastry

3 3/4 c. sifted flour	**2 tbsp. shortening**
1 tsp. salt	**3/4 c. (about) ice water**
1 c. cold butter	

Combine the flour and salt in a bowl and cut in the butter and shortening until particles are fine. Add water, 1 tablespoon at a time, to make a stiff dough. Cover and chill.

Duxelles

1 lb. mushrooms, finely chopped	**2 tsp. flour**
1/4 c. chopped green onion	**Dash of pepper**
1/4 c. butter	**1/4 c. beef broth**
1/2 tsp. salt	**2 tbsp. chopped parsley**
1/4 tsp. marjoram	**1/2 c. finely chopped cooked ham**

Saute the mushrooms and onion in butter in a saucepan until liquid evaporates. Stir in salt, marjoram, flour, pepper and broth. Cook, stirring constantly, until mixture comes to a boil and thickens. Remove from heat and stir in parsley and ham. Cool.

Tomatoes with Horseradish Cream

8 sm. tomatoes	**1/2 tsp. Dijon mustard**
1/2 c. whipping cream	**Dash of salt**
1 tbsp. horseradish	

Cut tops from the tomatoes and hollow out slightly, scooping out seeds. Drain upside down. Whip the cream until stiff and fold in horseradish, mustard and salt. Fill the tomatoes with cream mixture just before serving. Serve around Beef Wellington.

Elegant Beef Wellington (page 56)

FLANK STEAK CASSEROLE

1 flank steak	1 tbsp. minced onion
1 tbsp. lemon juice	1 c. bread crumbs
1 1/2 tsp. salt	1 c. tomatoes
Dash of pepper, nutmeg and cloves	1 pt. hot water or tomato juice

Score the steak on both sides and sprinkle with the lemon juice, salt, pepper, nutmeg and cloves. Combine the onion, bread crumbs and tomatoes, mix well and spread over the steak. Roll as for jelly roll and tie with string. Brown in a small amount of fat in a skillet. Add the water and cover skillet. Bake in 350-degree oven for 2 hours. Thicken the liquid for gravy, if desired. 8 servings.

Mrs. Myrtle Allanson, Charles City, Virginia

GINGER BEEF

1 1/4 lb. flank steak	1 1/2 tsp. salt
2 onions, chopped	3 tbsp. salad oil
3 cloves of garlic, minced	1 1-lb. can tomatoes
1 1/2 tsp. turmeric	1 10-oz. can onion soup
1/4 tsp. dried chili pepper	4 c. cooked rice
5 tbsp. ginger	Pickled watermelon

Cut the steak into 2 x 1/2-inch strips. Combine the onions, garlic, turmeric, chili pepper, ginger and salt in a bowl and add the steak. Refrigerate for about 3 hours. Heat the oil in a Dutch oven and add the steak mixture. Cook until browned, then add the tomatoes. Cook over high heat for 10 minutes. Add the soup and cover. Simmer for 1 hour and 30 minutes to 2 hours or until steak is tender. Serve with rice and garnish with pickled watermelon.

Mrs. W. M. Carlock, Shreveport, Louisiana

PARSLIED RIB STEAKS

2 rib steaks	1/2 c. chopped shallots
1 tbsp. olive oil	Pepper to taste
6 tbsp. butter	1 tbsp. chopped parsley

Remove all fat from the steaks. Rub steaks with olive oil and place in a broiler pan. Broil on each side for 2 minutes. Cream the butter, shallots, parsley and pepper together and spread in a baking dish. Place the steaks on the butter mixture and cover tightly. Place the baking dish over a saucepan of boiling water for about 6 minutes. Serve the steaks with creamed potatoes. 2 servings.

Mrs. R. K. Jeffries, Alexandria, Louisiana

BEEF WITH HORSERADISH

4 cubed beef steaks	1/2 c. cooking sherry or broth
1 lge. onion, sliced	1 c. sour cream
2 tbsp. butter or margarine	2 tsp. prepared horseradish
Salt and pepper to taste	2 tsp. chopped dill or dillseed
2 tbsp. soy sauce	

Brown the steaks and onion lightly in butter in a skillet. Add the salt, pepper, soy sauce and sherry and cover. Simmer for 20 minutes. Combine the sour cream, horseradish and dill and stir into the steak mixture. Heat through and serve on rice.

Mrs. A. J. Houdek, Sorrento, Florida

STUFFED ROUND STEAK

4 slices bacon, diced	2 1/2 lb. thin round steak
1 onion, chopped	1/2 tsp. salt
1 1/2 c. toasted bread cubes	1/8 tsp. pepper
2 tbsp. minced parsley	1 c. bouillon
1/2 tsp. celery salt	1 8-oz. can tomato sauce
1/4 tsp. sage	

Cook the bacon and onion in a saucepan until the bacon is crisp. Add the bread cubes, parsley, celery salt and sage and mix well. Cut the steak into 5 portions and season with salt and pepper. Spread each portion of steak with the bacon mixture. Roll as for jelly roll and secure with toothpicks. Place in a large skillet and add the bouillon. Cover and simmer for 1 hour. Add the tomato sauce and cover. Simmer for 45 minutes or until steak is done. Uncover and cook until liquid is thickened. Garnish with parsley.

Nancy Cross, Harrison, Arkansas

PLANKED T-BONE STEAK

1 T-bone steak	Chopped chives
Tomatoes	Grated Parmesan cheese

Place the steak on rack of a broiler pan. Broil to desired degree of doneness, then place on a heated plank. Cut the tomatoes in half crosswise. Place around steak and sprinkle with chives and Parmesan cheese. Broil until cheese is melted.

Planked T-Bone Steak (above)

STEAK AND OLIVES

2 tbsp. salad oil
1 1/2 lb. round steak, 3/4 in. thick
1 med. onion, chopped

1/2 green pepper, chopped
1 3 1/3-oz. jar stuffed olives
1 can cream of tomato soup

Heat the oil in a heavy skillet. Cut the steak into serving pieces, then brown with the onion and green pepper in hot oil. Slice the olives and add olives and brine to the steak mixture. Add the tomato soup and cover tightly. Cook over low heat for 1 hour and 30 minutes or until steaks are tender. May be baked at 350 degrees for about 2 hours. 6 servings.

Mrs. J. A. Satterfield, Forth Worth, Texas

GRILLED DILL STEAK

3/4 c. olive oil
3/4 c. dill pickle liquid
1/3 c. sliced dill pickles
1 clove of garlic, minced

1 3-lb. beef top round, 2 in.
   thick
Salt and pepper to taste

Combine the oil, pickle liquid, pickles and garlic in a large, shallow dish. Add the beef, turn until coated and cover. Marinate in refrigerator overnight, turning once. Drain beef and reserve marinade. Place beef on rack in a broiler pan. Broil 6 inches from heat for 14 to 17 minutes on each side for medium doneness, brushing with reserved marinade frequently. Sprinkle the beef with salt and pepper. Place on a platter and pour pan juices over beef. Cut beef diagonally across grain into thin slices. 8 servings.

Photograph for this recipe on page 10.

BUTTERED PLANKED STEAK

4 1/2 lb. sirloin steak 2 1/2
   in. thick
7 tbsp. butter
4 c. mashed potatoes

Salt and pepper to taste
2 tsp. chopped parsley
Juice of 1/2 lemon
Cooked buttered cauliflower

Preheat oven to 500 degrees. Place the steak on a broiler rack. Broil for 15 minutes, then remove to a hickory-seasoned plank. Reduce temperature to 350 degrees. Bake the steak for 1 hour. Brush edges of plank with 4 tablespoons butter and decorate with a ring of mashed potatoes. Season the steak with salt and pepper. Mix remaining butter with parsley and lemon juice and spread over steak. Garnish with bouquets of buttered cauliflower.

Mary Knox, Pegram, Tennessee

BROILED SIRLOIN STEAK WITH GARLIC SAUCE

3 tbsp. butter
1 tsp. garlic powder
3 tbsp. Worcestershire sauce

1/2 c. steak sauce
2 1/2 lb. sirloin steak

Melt the butter in a saucepan over low heat. Add the garlic powder, Worcestershire sauce and steak sauce and stir until mixed. Bring to boiling point and remove from heat. Place the steak on a broiler pan and brush with the steak sauce mixture. Broil 3 inches from heat for 5 minutes. Turn steak and brush with steak sauce mixture. Broil for 5 minutes longer. 4 servings.

Edna S. Denby, Fayetteville, North Carolina

SHERRY-BAKED STEAK

1 stick margarine	4 T-bone or sirloin steaks
1/2 c. sherry	Salt and pepper to taste

Melt the margarine in sherry in a saucepan over low heat. Place the steaks in a baking pan and add salt and pepper. Baste with the sherry mixture and cover with foil. Bake at 450 degrees for about 45 minutes, turning once and basting with sherry mixture frequently.

Mrs. Bobbie Bolding Pace, Pickens, South Carolina

HERB AND WINE-MARINATED STEAK

1 2/3 c. Burgundy	3/4 tsp. instant minced garlic
1/2 c. salad oil	1/4 tsp. ground pepper
2 tbsp. instant minced onion	3 lb. round steak, 2 1/2 in. thick
2 tsp. thyme leaves	1 7/8-oz. package brown gravy
2 tsp. salt	mix (opt.)

Combine the Burgundy, oil, onion, thyme, salt, garlic and pepper and mix well. Place the steak in a pan and pour Burgundy mixture over steak. Marinate for at least 18 hours in refrigerator, turning occasionally. Drain steak and reserve marinade. Grill steak over hot coals for 15 to 20 minutes on each side or to desired doneness. Strain reserved marinade and combine with 1 cup water and gravy mix in a saucepan. Bring to boiling point, stirring constantly, and cook until slightly thickened. Serve with steak. Garnish steak with canned peach halves pierced with whole cloves, if desired. 6 servings.

Herb and Wine-Marinated Steak (above)

Herbed Pork Roast (page 76)

pork

A Southern homemaker has experienced the joys of using pork in everyday meal planning all her life.

Pork is a meat most Southerners like to think of as friendly. Southern cooks turn especially to pork on those special occasions when family and friends get together. For example, during the summer pork is a favorite meat for outdoor barbecuing, especially on such festive days as the Fourth of July. And when the heat of summer days is replaced by the cool winds of autumn, Southern homemakers again put pork to use by serving hams and pork roasts. Even in the springtime, pork shows its versatility as a basic main course in Southern homes. An Easter meal, for instance, usually is not complete without a ham or other pork entree.

Pork might be called the meat for all seasons. Members of Southern families never tire of menus containing this versatile food. And like beef, fresh pork is available at your supermarket all year long.

As a homemaker, you are already familiar with many ways to prepare pork. By reading the following recipes, you can expand your knowledge of pork's versatility. You will enjoy discovering what excitingly different entrees can be prepared from every cut of pork. Countless pork ideas are yours for the reading.

Pork, fresh or cured, is a great favorite with American families. It is in best supply — and therefore is a better buy — during late fall and winter. Pork's delightful taste, ranging from the smoky goodness of hickory-cured ham to the delicate flavor of roast pork, is one reason for its long-time popularity. The quality of fresh pork can be measured by the fat and the color of the meat. High-quality fresh pork has an exterior well-covered with a fairly firm, half-inch layer of white fat. Meat from young animals is grayish-pink; in older animals it turns to pale rose. But the meat is always well-marbled with fat and is firm and fine-grained.

The best way to tell the quality of cured pork is to depend on brand name. Each meat packer has his own way of curing and smoking pork. To find the

general directions
FOR PORK

most appealing flavor and the most consistent quality, the products of several different meat packers should be sampled.

All cuts of pork will be tender. So, the dry heat methods of cooking are most often used. Large, chunky cuts of fresh and cured pork may be roasted — 350 degrees F for fresh pork, 300 degrees F for cured. Pork roast needs no special seasoning. But its delicious flavor may be enhanced by careful use of herbs and spices. Try making five or six stabs in the roast with the tip of a paring knife. Stuff each hole with slivers of garlic. Or, rub an uncooked roast with a mixture of 1 tablespoon salt, 1 tablespoon paprika, 1 teaspoon dry mustard, and 1/4 teaspoon ground ginger.

Sliced cured ham, bacon, and sausage may be panfried or broiled. Pork chops, cutlets, sliced fresh ham or pork shoulder, and sliced pork liver may be panfried. However, these cuts of pork are usually thin and panfrying may dry them out. To avoid this, they should be braised — browned on both sides and then cooked thoroughly in a small amount of liquid. Pork absorbs the flavor of the liquid in which it is cooked and braising in different liquids will produce many unusual flavor combinations. Orange juice, tomato juice, stewed tomatoes, bouillon, or cranberry juice are most frequently used.

It is important to cook every pork cut thoroughly. Some pork may contain small parasites; the long cooking process will kill any such organisms. The cooked meat of fresh pork should be grayish-white without the slightest tinge of pink. Cured pork will have a characteristic greyish-pink appearance. And, of course, just-cooked pork is always served on a heated platter to keep the meat piping hot and juicy.

RETAIL PORK CUTS AND HOW TO COOK THEM

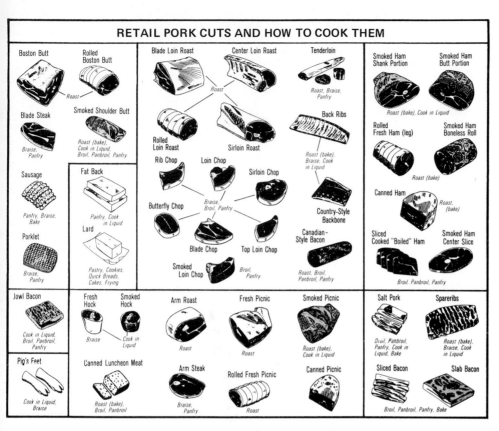

TIMETABLE FOR COOKING PORK

CUT	ROASTED AT 300 - 350 F. OVEN TEMPERATURE		BROILED	BRAISED
	Meat Thermometer Reading Degrees F.	Time Minutes Per lb.	Total Time Minutes	Total Time Hours
FRESH				
Loin				
Center	185	35 to 40		
Ends	185	45 to 50		
Shoulder				
Rolled	185	40 to 45		
Boston Butt	185	45 to 50		
Leg or Ham	185	30 to 35		
Chops				3/4 to 1
Spareribs				1 1/2
SMOKED				
Ham				
Whole	160	18 to 20		
Half	160	22 to 25		
Shank portion	160	35 to 40		
Butt portion	160	35 to 40		
Ham Slice				
(1/2 inch)			10 to 12	
(1 inch)			16 to 20	
Picnic	170	35		
Shoulder Butt	170	35		
Bacon			4 to 5	

65

Southern Baked Ham (below)

GLAZED LOUISIANA YAM AND HAM

6 med. yams	1/3 c. butter or margarine
2 c. dark corn syrup	1/2 tsp. seasoned salt
Lemon juice	1 5-lb. cooked bone-in half ham
Dash of pepper	4 unpeeled tart red apples
1/4 tsp. nutmeg	1/2 c. walnut halves

Place the yams in a saucepan, cover with boiling, salted water and cook for about 30 minutes or until just tender. Drain, peel and cut in half. Place in a shallow 2 1/2-quart baking dish. Blend the corn syrup, 1 tablespoon lemon juice, pepper and nutmeg and reserve 1/2 cup of the mixture for basting ham. Pour remaining corn syrup mixture over yams and dot yams with butter. Sprinkle with seasoned salt and set aside. Place ham in a shallow roasting pan. Bake in 325-degree oven for 1 hour and 45 minutes. Core the apples and cut into 1/4-inch thick slices. Brush with lemon juice. Add the apple slices and walnuts to yam mixture. Remove ham from oven and brush with reserved corn syrup mixture. Bake ham and yam mixture for about 25 minutes longer, basting both occasionally. 6 servings.

BAKED CANADIAN BACON

2 lb. unsliced Canadian bacon	1/2 tsp. dry mustard
1/2 c. brown sugar	1/2 c. pineapple juice

Place the Canadian bacon in a baking pan. Combine the brown sugar, mustard and pineapple juice and pour half the mixture over Canadian bacon. Bake at 325 degrees for 1 hour, basting every 15 minutes. 4 servings.

Ruby Ray Evans, Post, Texas

SOUTHERN BAKED HAM

1 c. apple cider	1 c. brown sugar
1 5-lb. ham	4 doz. cloves

1 can cherry pie filling	**1/2 c. orange juice**
1/2 c. raisins	

Mix the apple cider with 1/2 cup water. Wash the ham and place in a kettle. Cover with cold water and bring to a boil. Simmer until tender. Remove from kettle and remove outside skin. Sprinkle with brown sugar and dot with cloves. Place in a baking pan. Bake in 350-degree oven for 1 hour, basting with cider mixture frequently. Mix remaining ingredients in a saucepan and bring to a boil. Remove from heat and serve with ham.

Vernie Bennett, Union Mills, North Carolina

CHINESE HAM BALLS WITH FRUITED GINGER SAUCE

1 lb. ground smoked ham	**1/2 c. orange juice**
1 lb. pork sausage	**1 tsp. grated orange rind**
1 tbsp. instant minced onion	**2 tbsp. cornstarch**
2 eggs	**1 tbsp. sugar**
1/2 c. dry bread crumbs	**1 tbsp. soy sauce**
1/2 c. milk	**1/2 tsp. powdered ginger**
1/2 tsp. powdered mustard	**1/4 c. vinegar**
1/2 c. water	**2 tbsp. butter**
1 No. 2 1/2 can fruit cocktail	**1/4 c. sherry**

Combine first 7 ingredients in a bowl and mix well. Shape into 2-inch balls. Brown on all sides in a skillet over low heat. Drain off excess fat and add water. Cover and cook for about 20 minutes. Drain the fruit cocktail, reserving 1 cup syrup. Combine fruit cocktail, reserved syrup and remaining ingredients in a saucepan and bring to boiling point over low heat, stirring frequently. Serve hot over Ham Balls. 8 servings.

Chinese Ham Balls with Fruited Ginger Sauce (above)

EGGPLANT LOUISE

1 med. eggplant	1/2 c. tomato soup
2 tbsp. chopped onion	1 1/2 c. cooked rice
Butter	1 1/2 c. ground cooked ham
2 tbsp. parsley	Bread crumbs

Cut the eggplant in half lengthwise and cook in salted water in a saucepan for 10 minutes. Scoop out pulp, leaving a shell 3/4 inch thick. Brown the onion in small amount of butter in a saucepan. Add 1 tablespoon parsley, tomato soup, eggplant pulp, rice and ham. Fill eggplant shells with the ham mixture and sprinkle with bread crumbs. Place in a baking pan and dot with butter. Bake for 30 minutes at 350 degrees. Sprinkle with remaining parsley and serve.

Mrs. Paul Knight, St. Cloud, Florida

HAM PATTIES WITH SOUR CREAM

2 c. ground cooked ham	2 eggs, slightly beaten
1 tbsp. grated onion	2 tbsp. butter
1/2 c. dry bread crumbs	1/4 c. water
1 1/2 tbsp. chopped parsley	1/2 tsp. paprika
1 tsp. prepared mustard	1 c. sour cream
1/8 tsp. salt	

Combine the ham, onion, bread crumbs, parsley, mustard and salt in a bowl. Add the eggs and blend well. Shape into patties and brown in butter, on both sides. Keep warm. Combine the water and paprika in a saucepan and heat to boiling point. Remove from heat and stir in sour cream. Spoon over ham patties and garnish with additional parsley, if desired.

Mrs. James T. Sowell, Montgomery, Alabama

HAMLETS

1/2 lb. ground ham	6 slices pineapple
3/4 tsp. dry mustard	3 c. mashed sweet potatoes
1/4 tsp. pepper	3 tbsp. butter
1/2 c. milk	Salt to taste

Combine the ham, mustard, pepper and 1/4 cup milk and mix well. Shape into 6 patties. Place the pineapple slices in a shallow baking pan and place ham patties on the pineapple. Combine remaining milk with remaining ingredients and place on ham patties. Bake for 20 minutes at 350 degrees. 6 servings.

Mrs. W. W. Whaley, Birmingham, Alabama

HAM CASSEROLE

1 c. cracker crumbs	1 lb. ground ham
1 c. butter, softened	1 med. onion, chopped

1 c. cooked rice

1 c. milk, scalded

3 eggs, beaten

1 tbsp. chopped green pepper

1 lb. grated cheese

Mix the cracker crumbs and butter and reserve 2/3 cup for topping. Press remaining crumb mixture in 1 1/2-quart baking dish. Combine the ham, onion and rice and spread over crumb mixture. Stir the milk into eggs slowly and add the green pepper and cheese. Pour over casserole and sprinkle with reserved crumb mixture. Bake at 325 degrees until heated through.

Mrs. Willie Hampton, Jefferson, Texas

FRIED HAM PATTIES

2 c. ground ham

1 egg, beaten

2/3 c. flour

1 1/2 tsp. baking powder

1 tsp. cinnamon

1 tsp. sugar

1/2 c. drained crushed pineapple

Combine all ingredients and mix well. Shape into patties and fry in deep, hot fat until golden brown on both sides.

Mrs. E. C. French, Bismarck, Arkansas

HAM CONES

1 lb. ground ham

1 tbsp. grated onions

1 tbsp. parsley flakes

2 tbsp. orange juice

1 tbsp. prepared mustard

1 egg

1/2 c. crushed corn flakes

Mix all ingredients except corn flakes and shape into cones. Roll in crushed corn flakes and place in a greased baking pan. Bake at 375 degrees for 45 minutes.

Mrs. Cecil B. Howard, Maryville, Tennessee

HAM LOAVES

1/2 c. (packed) dark brown sugar

1 tsp. dry mustard

1/4 c. vinegar

1/4 c. water

2 c. ground cooked ham

1 egg, beaten

1 c. crushed corn flakes

1/2 c. milk

Combine first 4 ingredients in a saucepan and heat until the sugar dissolves. Combine remaining ingredients and shape into 6 loaves. Place in a baking pan. Bake at 350 degrees for 1 hour, basting frequently with the mustard sauce.

Mrs. Erling Grovenstein, Jr., Atlanta, Georgia

Ham and Sweet Potato Casserole (below)

HAM AND SWEET POTATO CASSEROLE

1 1/2 c. cubed cooked ham	1 9-oz. package frozen cut
1/2 c. sliced celery	green beans
4 tbsp. butter or margarine	1 c. mashed sweet potatoes
1 tsp. dry mustard	1 tsp. grated lemon rind
1 10 1/2-oz. can mushroom gravy	

Brown the ham and celery in 2 tablespoons butter in a saucepan. Add the
mustard and mushroom gravy. Cook the beans according to package directions
and drain. Add to the ham mixture, mix well and pour into a 1-quart casserole.
Combine the sweet potatoes, remaining butter and lemon rind and mix well.
Spoon around edge of casserole. Bake at 350 degrees for 30 minutes or until
heated through. 4 servings.

RICE AND HAM RING

2 c. cooked rice	1/2 c. milk
1 c. diced cooked ham	1/4 tsp. salt
1 egg	1/2 tsp. dried basil
2/3 c. mushroom soup	1 c. crushed potato chips

Preheat oven to 375 degrees. Combine the rice and ham. Combine remaining
ingredients and beat well. Place alternate layers of the ham mixture and soup

mixture in a greased 9-inch ring mold and sprinkle with potato chips. Place in a pan in 1 inch of hot water. Bake for about 30 minutes. 6 servings.

Jacqueline Huffman, New Castle, Virginia

HAM TIMBALES WITH BECHAMEL SAUCE

4 eggs, lightly beaten	1 c. chopped ham
1 c. milk	2 tbsp. butter
1 1/2 tsp. salt	3 tbsp. flour
3/4 tsp. pepper	1 c. hot meat stock
1/2 tsp. paprika	1/2 c. cream
1 tsp. onion juice	

Combine the eggs, milk, 1 teaspoon salt, 1/2 teaspoon pepper, 1/4 teaspoon paprika, onion juice and ham and mix well. Pour into buttered molds and place greased paper over top. Place in pan of hot water. Bake for 25 minutes at 350 degrees. Melt the butter in a saucepan. Add flour and brown. Add the meat stock and cook, stirring, until thick and smooth. Add the cream and remaining salt, pepper and paprika and heat through. Serve with Ham Timbales.

Mrs. C. B. Bushager, Del Rio, Texas

HAM AND CHEESE FONDUE

3 c. cubed French bread	3 tbsp. melted butter
3 c. cubed cooked ham	4 eggs, well beaten
1 c. cubed Cheddar cheese	3 c. milk
3 tbsp. flour	Hot sauce to taste
1 tbsp. dry mustard	

Place alternate layers of bread, ham and cheese in a 2-quart casserole. Mix the flour and mustard and sprinkle over cheese. Drizzle butter over the flour mixture. Mix the eggs, milk and hot sauce and pour over top. Cover and chill for at least 4 hours or overnight. Bake in 350-degree oven for 1 hour and serve at once. 6 servings.

Mrs. C. M. Mize, Lakeland, Florida

APPLE-HAM CASSEROLE

3 c. cooked diced ham	1/2 c. brown sugar
2 tbsp. prepared mustard	1 tsp. grated orange rind
2 apples, cored and sliced	2 tbsp. flour
2 tbsp. lemon juice	

Place the ham in a 1 1/2-quart casserole and spread with mustard. Place the apples over ham and sprinkle with lemon juice. Combine the brown sugar, orange rind and flour and sprinkle over apples. Bake at 350 degrees for 30 to 35 minutes. 4 servings.

Mrs. J. L. Stringfield, Cottageville, South Carolina

HAM AND POTATOES AU GRATIN

1 1/2 c. diced cooked ham	2 c. milk
3 c. diced cooked potatoes	Seasoned salt and pepper to taste
4 tbsp. margarine	1/2 c. grated sharp Cheddar cheese
1 sm. onion, minced	2 tbsp. fine dry bread crumbs
3 tbsp. flour	

Layer the ham and potatoes in a shallow 1 1/2-quart baking dish. Melt 3 tablespoons margarine in a saucepan. Add the onion and cook until golden. Blend in flour. Add milk gradually and cook, stirring, until thickened. Season with salt and pepper. Pour over the ham mixture and sprinkle with cheese and bread crumbs. Dot with remaining margarine. Bake in 400-degree oven for about 20 minutes. 4 servings.

Mrs. F. J. McGee, Dallas, Texas

HAM-CORN BREAD SHORTCAKE

1/2 c. bacon drippings	1/2 c. chopped peanuts
1/2 c. flour	4 c. diced cooked ham
4 c. milk	Salt to taste
2 tbsp. onion juice	Corn bread squares
1/2 c. diced cooked celery	Chopped parsley

Heat the bacon drippings in a saucepan and stir in the flour. Add the milk slowly and cook, stirring, until thickened. Add the onion juice, celery, peanuts, ham and salt and heat thoroughly. Split squares of hot corn bread and place creamed ham between layers and on top. Garnish with parsley.

Mrs. C. H. Parker, Eagle Lake, Florida

HAM PIE

2 tbsp. margarine	1 c. cooked peas and carrots
2 tbsp. flour	1 c. cubed boiled potatoes
1 c. milk	2 tbsp. parsley (opt.)
1/4 tsp. salt	2 tbsp. chopped canned mushrooms
1/8 tsp. pepper	6 unbaked cheese biscuits
Dash of paprika	1 tbsp. grated Parmesan cheese
1 1/2 c. cubed cooked ham	

Melt the margarine in a saucepan. Add the flour and stir until blended. Add the milk slowly and cook over medium heat, stirring, until thick. Add the seasonings. Place alternate layers of ham, peas and carrots, potatoes and white sauce in a greased 2-quart casserole and sprinkle with parsley and mushrooms. Place biscuits on top and sprinkle with cheese. Bake at 425 degrees for 30 minutes or until biscuits are lightly browned.

Mrs. Wilbur C. Johnson, Warrenton, Georgia

Plantation-Style Ham Slices (below)

PLANTATION-STYLE HAM SLICES

1 1/2-lb. cooked ham slices
1 can Compliment for ham

Place the ham slices in a shallow baking dish and cover with Compliment. Bake at 350 degrees for 35 minutes. 4 servings.

BARBECUED HAM

6 slices boiled ham
2 tbsp. butter
1 tbsp. vinegar
1/4 tsp. dry mustard

1/4 tsp. salt
1/4 tsp. pepper
1/2 tsp. paprika

Brown the ham in butter in a skillet, then push to 1 side. Blend remaining ingredients into butter in skillet. Place the ham in vinegar mixture and cook for 2 minutes. Serve hot over crisp, buttered toast.

Ham Sauce

1/2 c. vinegar
1/2 c. sugar
4 tbsp. dry mustard

Salt to taste
3 egg yolks, beaten
1 pt. cream

Heat the vinegar in a saucepan and stir in dry ingredients. Stir into egg yolks slowly, then return to saucepan. Add the cream and cook over low heat until thickened.

Mrs. Earnest Johnson, Jacksonville, Alabama

HAM WITH BREAD STUFFING

2 eggs	1/2 tsp. pepper
1 c. milk	1/2 tsp. salt
4 c. fresh bread cubes	1 tbsp. grated onion
1/2 tsp. celery salt	2 center-cut ham slices
2 tbsp. melted margarine	Brown sugar

Beat the eggs in a bowl and add the milk. Add the bread cubes and let soak for several minutes. Add the celery salt, margarine, pepper, salt and onion and blend thoroughly. Spread between ham slices and sprinkle brown sugar over top. Place in a baking pan. Bake for 30 minutes at 350 degrees and garnish with crab apples and parsley.

Mrs. Ida Mae Banks, Tuscaloosa, Alabama

BOILED HAM WITH RAISIN SAUCE

4 to 6 slices country-cured ham	3/4 c. sugar
1 tsp. whole cloves	1 tbsp. cornstarch
1/2 c. seeded raisins	1 tbsp. butter
1/4 c. chopped citron (opt.)	1/2 tsp. lemon juice

Place the ham and cloves in a saucepan and add enough water to cover. Bring to a boil and reduce heat. Cover and simmer for 40 to 50 minutes or until ham is tender. Drain and trim. Simmer the raisins and citron in 1 cup boiling water in a saucepan for about 1 hour or until raisins are tender. Sift sugar and cornstarch together and add to raisin mixture, stirring constantly. Cook, stirring constantly, for 10 minutes. Remove from heat and add butter and lemon juice. Serve over ham slices.

Mrs. Phil Ingle, Granite Falls, North Carolina

STUFFED HAM ROLL

1 1/2 c. broken macaroni	Pepper to taste
6 c. boiling water	1 tsp. powdered sage
Salt	1 beaten egg
2 c. bread crumbs	1/2 c. evaporated milk
1 onion, chopped	2 ham slices, 1/2 in. thick

Cook the macaroni in 6 cups boiling water and 1 teaspoon salt in a saucepan until tender. Drain and rinse with cold water. Mix in bread crumbs, onion, salt to taste, pepper and sage. Add the egg and milk and spread between slices of ham. Roll up and tie securely with string. Place in a baking pan and add 1/4 cup water. Cover. Bake at 375 degrees for 45 minutes. Remove cover and bake for 20 minutes longer.

Mrs. Ernest Lee, Montgomery, Alabama

BAKED HAM WITH BLACK CHERRY SAUCE

1　2 1/2-lb. slice precooked ham, 　　1 1/2 in. thick	2 tsp. cornstarch Dash of salt
1　1-lb. can pitted dark sweet 　　red cherries	1 tbsp. chopped candied ginger 2 tsp. lemon juice

Slash the fat edge of ham and place in a shallow baking dish. Bake at 350 degrees for 40 to 45 minutes. Drain the cherries and reserve syrup. Add enough water to reserved syrup to make 1 cup liquid and stir into cornstarch gradually. Place in a saucepan and add cherries, salt and ginger. Cook, stirring constantly, until thickened, then cook for 2 minutes longer. Stir in lemon juice and serve over the ham. 6 servings.

Mrs. Jim Christie, Marked Tree, Arkansas

LOIN OF PORK WITH KRAUT AND APPLES

1　3-lb. loin pork roast, scored	1/2 c. sliced celery
Garlic salt and pepper to taste	3 1/2 c. sauerkraut
Marjoram and paprika to taste	1/3 c. (firmly packed) light
Flour	brown sugar
1/4 c. butter or margarine	1/4 c. chopped parsley
1 lge. onion, chopped	2 med. red tart apples

Sprinkle the pork roast with seasonings and coat with flour. Place on rack in a shallow roasting pan. Bake in 350-degree oven for 2 hours or until done. Melt the butter in a large skillet over medium heat and saute the onion for 2 minutes. Add the celery and cook for 1 minute longer. Mix in the sauerkraut, sugar and parsley. Core the apples and cut in wedges. Mix with onion mixture and cover. Simmer for 5 minutes or until apples are just tender and serve with roast pork. 6-8 servings.

Loin of Pork with Kraut and Apples (above)

PORK TENDERLOIN WITH SWEET POTATOES AND APPLES

1 lge. pork tenderloin	4 peeled apples, cored
1 c. milk	4 tsp. sugar
1/4 c. flour	4 tsp. seedless raisins
Salt and pepper to taste	4 sweet potatoes, quartered
1/2 tbsp. melted fat	4 marshmallows

Dip the pork in milk. Mix the flour with salt and pepper and dredge pork with flour mixture. Brown in fat in a Dutch oven. Fill center of apples with sugar and raisins and place sweet potatoes and apples around pork. Add remaining milk and cover. Cook over low heat for 1 hour and 15 minutes or until tenderloin is done. Place marshmallow on each apple just before serving.

Mrs. Herman A. Wolff, King, North Carolina

PORK SHOULDER WITH SAVORY STUFFING

1 5 to 6-lb. fresh pork shoulder	2 tbsp. fat
Salt and pepper to taste	2 c. soft bread crumbs
1/4 c. diced celery and tops	1/4 tsp. savory
1 tbsp. diced onion	Flour
1 tbsp. chopped parsley	

Remove skin and bones from pork shoulder and sprinkle inside with salt and pepper. Saute the celery, onion and parsley in fat in a saucepan until tender. Add the bread crumbs, savory, salt and pepper and stir until well mixed. Place the stuffing in cavity of pork shoulder and tie pork shoulder with string. Sprinkle with salt, pepper and flour and place, fat side up, on rack in a shallow baking pan. Roast at 325 degrees for about 4 hours or until tender, turning occasionally. Remove string and serve.

Mrs. Julias Childers, Cullman, Alabama

HERBED PORK ROAST

1 5-lb. pork loin	1/2 c. apple jelly
Salt and pepper to taste	2 tbsp. dry sauterne
Crushed thyme leaves to taste	3 tbsp. flour
Crushed marjoram leaves to taste	1/2 c. milk

Trim the fat on pork loin to 1/8 inch and sprinkle loin with seasonings. Place in a shallow baking pan. Roast in 325-degree oven for 1 hour and 45 minutes. Simmer the apple jelly and sauterne in a small saucepan over medium heat for 3 minutes, stirring frequently. Brush loin with some of the jelly mixture and roast for 1 hour and 15 minutes longer, basting occasionally with remaining jelly mixture. Remove loin to a heated serving platter. Pour off drippings from baking pan and skim off fat. Return 1/2 cup drippings to baking pan and place over low heat. Blend in flour, then add 1 1/2 cups water and milk. Cook for 2 minutes, stirring frequently, and season with salt and pepper. 8-10 servings.

Photograph for this recipe on page 62.

SPANISH ROAST PORK WITH OLIVES AND RICE

1 4-lb. pork loin	3/4 c. sliced stuffed olives
3 cloves of garlic, slivered	2 tbsp. cornstarch
5 1/2 c. chicken broth	1 c. rice
3/4 c. dry vermouth	2 tbsp. butter or margarine
1/2 tsp. ground sage	1/2 tsp. salt
1/4 tsp. pepper	1/4 tsp. crushed saffron

Score fat side of the pork and insert garlic in slits. Place in a shallow roasting pan. Combine 1 1/2 cups broth, vermouth, sage and pepper and pour over pork. Roast in 325-degree oven for 1 hour and 20 minutes, basting occasionally. Add 1/2 cup olives to roasting pan and roast for 1 hour longer. Place the pork on a platter and keep warm. Remove olives from pan with slotted spoon and reserve. Skim excess fat from pan liquid and add enough water to make 1 3/4 cups liquid. Bring to a boil. Blend the cornstarch and 1/4 cup water, stir into boiling liquid and cook for 30 seconds, stirring constantly. Remove from heat and serve with pork. Combine the rice, remaining chicken broth, butter, salt and saffron in a large saucepan. Bring to a boil, stir well and cover. Cook over low heat for 15 to 20 minutes or until rice is tender and add reserved olives and remaining olives. Serve with pork and gravy.

BARBECUED PORK

1 pork shoulder roast	1/2 c. catsup
1 tsp. salt	1/2 tsp. chili powder
1 tsp. celery seed	1/2 tsp. nutmeg
1/8 tsp. cinnamon	1 tsp. sugar
1/3 c. vinegar	1 c. water

Brown the roast in small amount of fat and place in a Dutch oven. Mix remaining ingredients in a saucepan and bring to a boil. Pour over roast and cover. Bake at 325 degrees until done, basting occasionally with drippings.

Mrs. Anna Mae Hammond, Russell Springs, Kentucky

ORANGE-GLAZED PORK

1 4-lb. pork loin	1 1/2 tsp. cornstarch
1 sm. onion, grated	1/2 tsp. ground ginger
1 tbsp. butter	1 c. orange juice
2 tbsp. brown sugar	1 tbsp. steak sauce

Place pork loin, fat side up, on rack in a roasting pan. Roast at 325 degrees for 1 hour and 30 minutes. Saute the onion in butter in a saucepan until soft. Stir in remaining ingredients and cook, stirring constantly, until thick. Brush over pork and roast for 1 hour longer, brushing every 15 minutes with onion mixture. 4 servings.

Mrs. Loyd A. Huffman, Wilkesboro, North Carolina

SWEET-SOUR PORK ROAST

1 3 1/2 to 4-lb. pork roast	1 tsp. grated lemon rind
Salt	2 tbsp. brown sugar
Pepper to taste	1/2 tsp. nutmeg or allspice
1 8-oz. can tomato sauce	1 No. 2 can pineapple chunks
2 tbsp. lemon or lime juice	1/2 c. seedless raisins
1/2 c. water	

Sprinkle the pork roast with salt to taste and pepper and place in a baking pan. Roast at 325 degrees for 1 hour and pour off excess fat. Combine the tomato sauce. lemon juice, water, grated rind, 1/2 teaspoon salt, brown sugar, and nutmeg in a saucepan. Drain the pineapple and reserve juice. Add reserved juice to tomato sauce mixture and stir well. Simmer for 10 minutes. Add raisins and pineapple chunks and pour over roast. Roast for about 2 hours, basting occasionally and adding water, if needed. 6 servings.

Pearl H. Wright, Hollywood, Florida

GLAZED PORK CHOPS

6 pork chops, cut 3/4 in. thick	1/4 tsp. cinnamon
1 tsp. salt	1/4 tsp. ginger
1/4 tsp. pepper	1/8 tsp. ground cloves
1 1-lb. can peach halves	2 tsp. flour
1/2 c. light corn syrup	1/4 c. water
1 tsp. lemon juice	

Brown the pork chops on both sides in a skillet over medium heat and pour off excess fat. Sprinkle pork chops with salt and pepper. Drain the peaches, reserving 1/4 cup syrup. Mix reserved peach syrup, corn syrup, lemon juice, cinnamon, ginger and cloves, pour over chops and cover. Cook over low heat for 45 minutes or until pork is done. Add the peach halves and heat through. Remove chops and peach halves to a serving platter and keep warm. Mix the flour and water and stir into the liquid in skillet. Bring to a boil, stirring constantly, then spoon over chops. 6 servings.

Glazed Pork Chops (above)

CANTON PORK CHOPS

6 pork chops, 1/2 in. thick	2 tbsp. honey
2 tbsp. bacon drippings	1 tsp. lemon juice
1 tsp. salt	1/4 tsp. cinnamon
1/2 tsp. pepper	1/2 tsp. ginger
1 16-oz. can sliced peaches	Flour

Brown the pork chops in bacon drippings in a skillet and pour off excess drippings. Season with salt and pepper. Drain the peaches, reserving 1/2 cup liquid. Combine reserved liquid with honey, lemon juice, cinnamon and ginger and pour over chops. Cover tightly. Cook over low heat for 45 minutes or until done. Add peach slices and cook until heated through. Remove the pork chops and peach slices to a warm serving platter. Thicken the liquid with flour for gravy and spoon over chops. 6 servings.

Melessia Morgan, Butler, Alabama

PORK CHOPS IN SOUR CREAM GRAVY

1 c. sliced mushrooms	1 c. water
2 tbsp. butter	1/2 tsp. Worcestershire sauce
4 pork chops	2 tbsp. flour
1 tsp. salt	1/2 c. sour cream
1/8 tsp. pepper	Paprika

Brown the mushrooms in butter in a heavy skillet and remove from skillet. Place the pork chops in the skillet and brown on both sides. Season with salt and pepper. Add 1/2 cup water, Worcestershire sauce and mushrooms and cover. Simmer for 40 minutes. Remove chops to a platter and keep warm. Mix the flour and remaining water and stir into liquid in skillet. Cook, stirring constantly, until thickened, then simmer for 5 minutes. Stir in the sour cream and pour over pork chops. Sprinkle with paprika.

Mrs. C. R. Fricks, Fort Smith, Arkansas

SWEET AND SOUR PORK CHOPS

2 tbsp. flour	1 green pepper, cut in strips
1 tsp. salt	1 onion, sliced
4 pork chops, 1 in. thick	2 tbsp. molasses
1 tbsp. bacon drippings	2 tsp. soy sauce
1 4-oz. can mushrooms	2 tbsp. vinegar

Mix the flour and 1/2 teaspoon salt and dredge pork chops with the flour mixture. Brown in bacon drippings in a skillet. Drain the mushrooms and reserve liquid. Add enough water to reserved liquid to make 1 cup liquid. Add to the pork chops, then add green pepper and onion. Sprinkle with remaining salt. Combine remaining ingredients and pour over chops. Cook over low heat for 45 minutes.

Mrs. Fred R. Lantz, Corpus Christi, Texas

STUFFED PORK CHOPS

6 pork chops, 1 1/2 in. thick	1/2 tsp. salt
1 c. cooked rice	1/4 tsp. poultry seasoning
2 tbsp. chopped green pepper	2 tbsp. shortening
2 tbsp. chopped onion	1 can Compliment for pork chops

Cut a pocket in the pork chops. Mix the rice, green pepper, onion, salt and poultry seasoning in a 2-quart bowl and stuff the pork chops. Brown chops in hot shortening in a 10-inch skillet, then place in a shallow 2-quart baking dish. Add Compliment and cover. Bake in 350-degree oven for 45 minutes or until tender. 6 servings.

Photograph for this recipe on page 2.

DIXIE PORK CHOPS

8 pork chops	2 tbsp. flour
1/2 tsp. salt	1 c. hot water
1/2 tsp. sage	1 tbsp. vinegar
4 cored tart apples, sliced	1/2 c. seedless raisins
1/4 c. brown sugar	

Brown the pork chops in small amount of fat in a skillet and sprinkle with salt and sage. Place in a baking dish and top with the apple rings. Sprinkle with brown sugar. Add the flour to fat in skillet and blend. Add the water and vinegar and cook until thick, stirring constantly. Add the raisins and pour over chops. Bake in 350-degree oven for 1 hour.

Mrs. Ned R. Mitchell, Charleston, South Carolina

CRANBERRY PORK CHOPS

4 loin pork chops, 1 in. thick	1/2 c. honey
Salt and pepper to taste	1/4 tsp. ground cloves
2 c. ground cranberries	1/4 tsp. ground nutmeg

Brown the pork chops in a skillet and season with salt and pepper. Mix the cranberries, honey, cloves and nutmeg and pour over chops. Cover. Bake at 300 degrees for about 1 hour or until tender. 4 servings.

Mrs. Louis Love, Miami, Florida

BARBECUED PORK CHOPS WITH LEMON

6 pork chops, cut 1 in. thick	1/2 c. catsup
Salt and pepper to taste	1/2 c. water
6 lemon slices	2 tbsp. brown sugar

Brown the pork chops in a heavy frypan and season with salt and pepper. Place lemon slice on each chop. Combine the catsup, water and brown sugar and pour over chops. Cover tightly. Bake in a 350-degree oven for about 45 minutes or until done. 6 servings.

Mrs. W. W. Smith, Alton, Virginia

STUFFED PORK CHOPS

4 thick pork chops	1/4 c. chopped onion
Salt and pepper	3 tbsp. butter or margarine
2 c. dry bread cubes	Flour
1 c. cracker crumbs	4 tbsp. oil
1/2 tsp. poultry seasoning	1 can mushroom soup
Sage to taste	

Cut a pocket in each pork chop and sprinkle pork chops with salt and pepper to taste. Combine the bread cubes, cracker crumbs, 1/8 teaspoon pepper, poultry seasoning and sage in a bowl. Cook the onion in butter until tender. Add to bread mixture and mix well. Add enough water to moisten. Fill pork chop pockets with bread mixture and secure with toothpicks. Dredge pork chops with flour and brown in oil in a skillet. Add the mushroom soup and cover skillet. Bake at 350 degrees for 1 hour.

Myrtle G. Haden, Gretna, Virginia

PORK CHOPS WITH ACORN CIRCLES

6 pork chops, 1 in. thick	12 whole cloves
2 tbsp. fat	12 cooked prunes
1 tsp. salt	6 cooked dried apricot halves
3 acorn squash	1/2 c. orange juice

Brown the pork chops in hot fat in a skillet and sprinkle with salt. Cut the squash crosswise in six 1-inch slices and remove seeds. Place a squash ring on each pork chop. Press the cloves into prunes and place 2 prunes and 1 apricot half in center of each squash ring. Add the orange juice and cover. Simmer for 45 minutes or until pork chops and squash are tender. 6 servings.

Mrs. E. R. Sanders, Athens, Georgia

PORK CHOPS AND DRESSING

1 onion, diced	4 slices dry bread
1 green pepper, diced	2 tsp. poultry seasoning
1 can chicken-noodle soup	6 pork chops
1 recipe baked corn bread	Salt and pepper to taste

Cook the onion and green pepper in the soup in a saucepan until tender. Add remaining ingredients except the pork chops, salt and pepper and place in a baking dish. Place pork chops on top and sprinkle with salt and pepper. Cover baking dish. Bake for 45 minutes in 400-degree oven. Uncover and bake for 15 minutes longer.

Mrs. A. H. Lindsey, Texas City, Texas

Pork Chops with Kraut and Baked Apples (below)

PORK CHOPS WITH KRAUT AND BAKED APPLES

3 1/4 c. drained sauerkraut	6 med. red apples
2 tsp. dried chopped chives	1/4 c. (firmly packed) brown sugar
1/4 tsp. dillweed	1/4 c. dark seedless raisins
6 loin pork chops, 1 in. thick	1 c. chicken broth or bouillon
Salt and pepper to taste	1 1/2 tbsp. flour
7 tbsp. melted butter or margarine	1/2 c. heavy cream

Combine the sauerkraut, chives and dillweed and place in a large, shallow baking dish. Sprinkle the pork chops with salt and pepper. Brown on both sides in 3 tablespoons butter in a skillet and place on sauerkraut mixture. Reserve 2 tablespoons pork drippings in skillet. Core the apples and pare 1 inch peeling from top of each apple. Combine 2 tablespoons butter with brown sugar and raisins and stuff apples. Place apples at each end of baking dish and brush tops with remaining butter. Pour chicken broth over chops and cover only the chops with aluminum foil. Bake in 350-degree oven for 1 hour, basting chops and apples with pan liquid. Remove foil from chops and bake for 20 minutes longer or until chops and apples are tender, basting occasionally. Drain and reserve 1 cup broth. Heat skillet with reserved drippings and stir in flour. Add reserved broth and boil for 1 minute, stirring constantly. Stir in cream and heat through, but do not boil. Serve with sauerkraut, chops and apples. 6 servings.

DELUXE PORK AND PEAS

2 tbsp. butter or margarine	1 8-oz. package noodles
4 c. cubed cooked pork	1 can cream of mushroom soup
3/4 c. water	1/4 tsp. pepper

1/2 c. sliced onions
1 c. sliced celery
1/2 tsp. dried thyme
2 tsp. salt

1 c. cooked peas
1/2 c. grated American cheese
1 c. buttered bread crumbs

Melt the butter in a large skillet. Add the pork and brown lightly. Add the water, onions, celery, thyme and 1 teaspoon salt and cover. Simmer for 20 minutes or until celery is tender. Cook the noodles according to package directions and drain. Add the pork mixture, soup, pepper, peas, cheese and remaining salt. Place in a greased 2-quart casserole and top with the bread crumbs. Bake at 350 degrees for 30 minutes. 6 servings.

Mrs. R. W. Graney, Charlotte, North Carolina

EGG NOODLES WITH PORK SAUCE

1 1/2 lb. boneless pork shoulder
Flour
1 tbsp. salad oil
1/2 c. chopped celery
1/2 c. chopped green pepper
1 clove of garlic, minced
Salt
1/2 tsp. monosodium glutamate
1/8 tsp. pepper

1 onion bouillon cube
1 1-lb. can green beans
1/2 c. sour cream
3 qt. boiling water
4 c. medium egg noodles
1/4 c. butter or margarine
1/2 tsp. caraway seed (opt.)
Paprika
Chopped parsley

Cut the pork into 2 x 1/2-inch strips and dredge with flour. Brown in hot oil in a large skillet and drain off excess fat. Add the celery, green pepper and garlic and cook for 3 minutes. Stir in 1 teaspoon salt, monosodium glutamate, pepper and bouillon cube. Drain the beans and reserve liquid. Add enough water to reserved liquid to make 1 cup liquid and add to pork mixture. Cover the skillet. Simmer for 40 to 45 minutes or until pork is tender. Stir in beans and sour cream and heat through. Add 1 tablespoon salt to boiling water and add noodles gradually so that water continues to boil. Cook, stirring occasionally, until tender and drain in a colander. Toss the noodles with butter and caraway seed. Serve pork mixture over noodles and garnish with paprika and parsley. 4-6 servings.

Egg Noodles with Pork Sauce (above)

SAVORY PORK DISH

2 lb. lean pork	2 tbsp. minced parsley
2 eggs, beaten	2 cloves of garlic, minced
1 tsp. salt	1/4 c. oil
1/4 tsp. pepper	2 c. water
1 c. bread crumbs	2 bouillon cubes

Cut the pork into bite-sized pieces. Combine the eggs, salt and pepper in a bowl. Mix the bread crumbs, parsley and garlic in a separate bowl. Dip pork into egg mixture, then dip into crumb mixture. Brown in the oil in a large skillet and remove from skillet. Drain the oil from skillet. Pour the water into skillet and add bouillon cubes. Simmer, stirring frequently, for 10 minutes. Stir into remaining egg mixture and heat through. Serve with pork. 6 servings.

Joyce Mumford, Arlington, Virginia

SWEET AND TANGY PORK

1 1/2 lb. boneless pork	1/4 c. vinegar
Seasoned flour	1/4 c. water
2 tbsp. salad oil	1 green pepper, cut into strips
1/2 c. bottled barbecue sauce	1 12-oz. jar pineapple preserves

Cut the pork into 1-inch cubes and coat with seasoned flour. Brown in the oil in a skillet. Add the barbecue sauce, vinegar and water and cover. Simmer for 45 minutes. Add the green pepper and preserves and cook for 15 minutes longer. 6 servings.

Mrs. Pat Allen, Little Rock, Arkansas

PORK TENDERLOIN IN SOUR CREAM

1 pork tenderloin, cut in strips	1 can sliced mushrooms
Salt and pepper to taste	1 can beef broth
Paprika to taste	1 c. sour cream
Butter	

Season the tenderloin with salt, pepper and paprika. Cook in small amount of butter in a skillet until golden. Add remaining ingredients and cover. Bake at 325 degrees for 1 hour and 30 minutes.

Mrs. Roy Van Hyning, Alexandria, Virginia

PORK STROGANOFF

1 can cream of celery soup	2 tbsp. chopped pimento
1/2 c. sour cream	1/4 tsp. salt
1/2 c. milk	Dash of pepper
1 c. cubed cooked pork	2 c. cooked noodles
2 tbsp. chopped parsley	2 tbsp. buttered bread crumbs

Blend the soup and sour cream. Stir in the milk, pork, parsley, pimento, seasonings and noodles. Pour into a 1 1/2-quart baking dish and top with the crumbs. Bake at 350 degrees for 30 minutes. 3-4 servings.

Mrs. Ione Dodson, Bremen, Georgia

CURRIED PORK WITH RICE

1 lb. rice	Salt and pepper to taste
1/2 lb. onions, cut in rings	1 tsp. curry powder
1/2 lb. pork, diced	Soy sauce to taste
1/2 c. butter	1 1/2 c. cooked mixed vegetables

Cook the rice in boiling water for about 12 minutes or until tender. Drain, rinse with cold water and drain well. Cook the onions and pork in half the butter in a skillet for about 15 minutes or until brown. Add remaining butter, half the rice, salt, pepper, curry powder, 1 cup water and soy sauce and cook over low heat, stirring frequently, until pork is tender. Add the mixed vegetables and remaining rice and mix well. Heat through, then place on a large heated plate. Garnish with slices of tomatoes. May serve with lettuce, cucumber and pickles.

Mrs. H. T. Bryant, Camden, Alabama

SUPER CHOP SUEY

1 lb. pork, cut in 1/2-in. cubes	1 tsp. salt
2 tbsp. fat	1/8 tsp. pepper
1 c. chopped celery	4 tbsp. soy sauce
1 c. sliced onions	1 No. 2 can bean sprouts
1 c. water	

Brown the pork in hot fat in a skillet. Add the celery, onions, water, salt, pepper, soy sauce and bean sprouts and cook for 15 minutes.

Tommy Bo Hannon, Lake Wales, Florida

BRAISED PORK

1 1/2 tbsp. tomato sauce	2 pork steaks, cut in strips
1 tbsp. lemon juice	1/2 sm. onion, sliced
1/4 tbsp. mustard	3 c. water
1/2 tsp. Worcestershire sauce	

Combine the tomato sauce, lemon juice, mustard and Worcestershire sauce. Add the pork and mix well. Brown in small amount of fat in a skillet. Top with onion slices and add water. Cover the skillet. Bake at 350 degrees for 1 hour. 2 servings.

Betty Ann Robinson, Erin, Tennessee

Lime Ribs (below)

LIME RIBS

1 3 to 4-lb. strip spareribs	1/2 tsp. coriander
3/4 c. lime juice	1/2 tsp. ginger
1/3 c. salad oil	1 1/2 tsp. salt
3 tbsp. brown sugar	1 lime, cut in wedges

Have spareribs sawed across rib bones so individual servings may be carved easily after baking. Combine the lime juice, salad oil, brown sugar, coriander, ginger and salt. Place spareribs in a shallow dish and pour lime mixture over spareribs. Cover and refrigerate for 6 to 8 hours. Drain spareribs and reserve marinade. Place spareribs, rib side up, on rack in a roasting pan and cover tightly. Bake at 350 degrees for 1 hour. Uncover and turn. Brush with reserved marinade and bake for 1 hour to 1 hour and 30 minutes longer, brushing with remaining marinade every 30 minutes. Remove spareribs to a heated platter, cut into servings and garnish with lime wedges. 4 servings.

BAKED PORK RIBS

3 lb. spareribs	1 tsp. cinnamon
Salt to taste	2 tbsp. brown sugar
4 apples	

Cut the spareribs in serving pieces and season with salt. Place in a roasting pan and cover tightly. Bake at 350 degrees for 1 hour and 30 minutes and pour off drippings. Core the apples and cut in 1/4-inch thick slices. Arrange slices around spareribs and sprinkle with cinnamon and brown sugar. Bake for 30 to 40 minutes longer. 4-6 servings.

Mrs. C. L. Blevins, Crumpler, North Carolina

TANGY STUFFED SPARERIBS

1 c. diced celery	1 1-lb. can jellied cranberry
1 med. onion, chopped	sauce
3 tbsp. butter or margarine	6 c. cubed dry bread
1 tsp. salt	2 2 1/2-lb. strips spareribs
Dash of pepper	2 tbsp. brown sugar
1/2 tsp. thyme	

Saute the celery and onion in butter in a saucepan for 3 minutes or until tender. Add the salt, pepper, thyme and 1/2 can cranberry sauce and mix well. Pour over the bread cubes and mix thoroughly. Place the spareribs in a shallow baking pan. Roast in 450-degree oven for 30 minutes and pour off drippings. Reduce temperature to 325 degrees. Turn 1 strip of spareribs, hollow side up, in pan and add the stuffing. Top with second strip of spareribs and secure with wooden picks. Roast for 1 hour. Mix remaining cranberry sauce and brown sugar and heat until melted. Spread on spareribs and roast for 30 minutes longer. 6 servings.

Mrs. Naomi H. Doosing, Cuero, Texas

CIDER PORK PIE

1 1/2 lb. boned country-style	1 tsp. salt
spareribs	5 tbsp. margarine
Seasoned flour	1 egg, separated
2 tbsp. shortening	Sage to taste
1/2 lb. cooking apples	Grated nutmeg to taste
1 lge. onion	5/8 c. cider
1 1/4 c. sifted flour	1 chicken bouillon cube

Preheat oven to 400 degrees. Cut the pork into small pieces and dredge with flour. Brown in shortening in a skillet. Peel and core apples and slice in thin rings. Cut onion in thin slices and separate into rings. Sift flour and salt into a bowl. Cut in the margarine until mixture resembles fine bread crumbs. Mix in egg yolk and enough cold water to make stiff pastry. Turn out onto floured board. Roll out and cut 1 inch larger than top of 1 1/2-quart casserole. Cut off a 1-inch strip of pastry from around edge of rolled pastry. Place half the pork in the casserole. Add half the apples and half the onion, seasoning with sage and nutmeg. Repeat layers. Heat cider in a saucepan and dissolve bouillon cube in cider. Pour into casserole. Press the 1-inch strip of pastry around top inner edge of the casserole and dampen with cold water. Place pastry on top. Seal edges to pastry strip and flute. Cut a slit in center of pastry for steam to escape and brush pastry with egg white. Bake for 30 minutes. Reduce temperature to 350 degrees and bake for about 20 minutes longer.

Ann Elsie Schmetzer, Madisonville, Kentucky

BAKED SPARERIBS

3 strips spareribs	Sage to taste
Flour	Prepared mustard
Salt and pepper to taste	4 tbsp. fat
Red pepper to taste	2 tbsp. flour

Cut spareribs in serving pieces and place on rack in a roasting pan. Dust with flour and add salt, peppers and sage. Spread layer of mustard on spareribs. Bake at 350 degrees for 1 hour and 30 minutes, basting several times. Drain and reserve 4 tablespoons fat. Place reserved fat in a frypan. Stir in the flour and cook until brown. Add 2 cups hot water and season with salt and pepper. Cook, stirring constantly, until thickened and serve with spareribs.

Mrs. William B. Marks, Harrisonburg, Virginia

KIDNEY BEANS WITH SPARERIBS

2 c. dried kidney beans	1/2 green pepper, chopped
1/3 lb. slab bacon	1/2 clove of garlic, chopped
1 tsp. salt	1 can beef consomme
1 1/2 lb. spareribs	1 carrot, grated
1 tbsp. fat	1/8 tsp. thyme
2 onions, chopped	1/4 tsp. pepper

Place the kidney beans in a saucepan, cover with water and soak overnight. Drain beans. Cut the bacon in 4 pieces and add to beans. Add the salt and 3 pints cold water and bring to a boil. Simmer for about 45 minutes. Cut the spareribs in serving pieces and brown in fat in a frypan. Add the onions, green pepper and garlic and cook for 3 minutes. Add the consomme, carrot, thyme and pepper and cook for 3 minutes longer. Drain liquid from beans and bacon and place in baking dish. Remove the spareribs from onion mixture and press into beans until half covered. Pour the onion mixture over bean mixture and cover the baking dish. Bake in 325-degree oven for about 1 hour.

Mrs. William B. Marks, Harrisonburg, Virginia

ORIENTAL SPARERIBS

2 lb. spareribs	3/4 tbsp. lemon juice
1 onion, chopped	1/3 tbsp. prepared mustard
1/3 clove of garlic, minced	3/4 tsp. salt
2 tbsp. oil	Pepper to taste
3/4 tbsp. vinegar	1/8 c. soy sauce
3/4 tbsp. honey	1/3 c. water

Cut the spareribs in serving pieces and place in a baking pan. Brown the onion and garlic in oil in a saucepan. Drain off oil and add remaining ingredients. Pour over spareribs. Bake at 325 degrees for about 1 hour, basting frequently.

Mrs. Bob Davis, Pecos, Texas

BARBECUED SPARERIBS WITH HERBS

6 lb. spareribs	1 tsp. thyme
3 qt. boiling water	1 c. dry red wine
2 whole cloves	1/3 c. catsup
1 med. onion	1 tbsp. soy sauce
1 tsp. salt	1/4 tsp. ginger
1 tsp. oregano	2 tbsp. honey
1 tsp. marjoram	1 clove of garlic, minced
1 tsp. rosemary	

Cut the spareribs in serving pieces and place in a deep kettle. Pour boiling water over the spareribs. Insert the cloves in onion and add to spareribs. Add the salt, oregano, marjoram, rosemary and thyme and bring to a boil. Reduce heat and cover. Simmer for about 50 minutes. Drain spareribs and arrange in shallow baking dish. Combine remaining ingredients and pour over spareribs. Broil 4 inches from heat for about 10 minutes on each side, basting frequently.

Mrs. W. W. Crowell, Nashville, Tennessee

JOHNNY MARZETTI

1 1/2 lb. ground lean pork	1 bunch celery, diced
8 lge. onions, sliced	2 green peppers, chopped
1/4 c. butter	Juice of 1/2 lemon
3 cans tomato soup	Salt and pepper
2 c. water	1 lb. sharp cheese, grated
1 lb. mushrooms, sliced	1 pkg. broad noodles

Brown the pork and onions in butter in a skillet. Add the soup, water, mushrooms, celery, green peppers, lemon juice, salt, pepper and cheese and simmer for 15 minutes. Cook the noodles in kettle of boiling, salted water until tender and drain. Mix with the pork mixture and cover. Cook over low heat for 1 hour, stirring occasionally. 12-16 servings.

Margaret Guy, Mt. Ulla, North Carolina

WON TON FRY

1/2 c. water	1/2 c. finely chopped celery
1 egg, beaten	1/2 c. bean sprouts, drained
6 c. flour	2 tbsp. soy sauce
1 1/2 c. ground pork	1/4 tsp. salt
1 tbsp. finely chopped green onion	1/4 tsp. pepper

Mix the water and egg in a mixing bowl and add the flour gradually. Knead on a floured surface for several minutes. Roll out about 1/2 cup dough at a time until very thin and cut in 2-inch squares. Combine remaining ingredients and place small amount in center of each square. Fold dough over and seal edges with a fork. Fry in deep, hot fat until brown.

Becky Elizabeth Wallace, Bartlesville, Oklahoma

DUKES MIXTURE

2 lb. ground pork, crumbled
1 can chicken with rice soup
1 pkg. noodles, cooked
1 green pepper, diced

1 sm. jar pimento, diced
1 can corn
1 lb. American cheese, grated
Buttered bread crumbs

Cook the pork in soup in a saucepan until done. Add remaining ingredients except crumbs and place in a casserole. Cover with crumbs. Bake for 30 minutes in 350-degree oven.

Mrs. Leo M. Fischer, East Gadsden, Alabama

WORSTER BRYER

6 lb. lean pork
Salt and pepper to taste
1 3/4 lb. rice

Ground cloves to taste
Allspice to taste
Red pepper to taste

Place the pork in a saucepan, cover with water and season with salt and pepper. Bring to a boil and reduce heat. Simmer until tender. Drain and reserve liquid. Bring reserved liquid to a boil and add the rice slowly. Cook until rice is tender. Grind the pork and add to rice. Season with the cloves, allspice and red pepper and cook until all water is absorbed, stirring constantly. Pour into pans and chill. Slice and fry in small amount of fat over low heat until brown.

Mrs. T. T. Walton, Bryan, Texas

PORK AND RICE-STUFFED SQUASH

3 acorn squash
Melted butter
1 lb. ground pork
1 c. cooked rice

1/2 c. water
Salt and pepper to taste
6 apple wedges
Cinnamon

Cut the squash in half, remove the seeds and brush with melted butter. Place in a shallow baking dish. Combine the pork, rice, water, salt and pepper, mix well and place in cavities of squash. Bake at 400 degrees for 45 minutes. Sprinkle the apple wedges with cinnamon and place on pork mixture. Bake for 15 minutes longer. 6 servings.

Mrs. C. L. Blevins, Crumpler, North Carolina

PORK AND NOODLE CASSEROLE

2 med. onions, chopped
1 bell pepper, chopped
2 tbsp. margarine
2 lb. ground pork shoulder
1 8-oz. package noodles

2 med. cans tomatoes
1 sm. can sliced mushrooms
1 tbsp. salt
1/2 lb. cheese, grated

Saute the onions and bell pepper in margarine in a saucepan until tender. Add the pork and cook, stirring constantly, until browned. Prepare the noodles according to package directions and drain. Add to the pork mixture. Add remaining ingredients and mix well. Place in a large casserole. Bake at 325 degrees for 1 hour, stirring occasionally. 12 servings.

Mrs. Alvah A. Hardy, Orlando, Florida

GUEST PORK

16 slices bacon	2 tsp. pepper
8 ground pork patties	Prepared mustard
4 tsp. seasoned salt	8 slices canned pineapple

Crisscross 2 slices of bacon and place a patty in center. Sprinkle with 1/2 teaspoon seasoned salt and 1/4 teaspoon pepper and spread with layer of mustard. Place a pineapple slice on top. Bring ends of bacon up over top and fasten with a toothpick. Repeat with remaining bacon, patties, seasonings and pineapple. Place in 8 x 12-inch baking dish. Bake at 350 degrees for 45 minutes.

Mrs. Mildred Sherrer, Bay City, Texas

AUTUMN DINNER

3 med. acorn squash	1 No. 2 can apple pie filling
18 baby link pork sausages	1/4 c. (firmly packed) brown sugar

Place whole squash in a baking pan. Bake in 350-degree oven for 20 minutes. Place sausage links on rack in a shallow baking pan and place in oven. Bake for 25 minutes longer. Remove sausage links and squash from oven. Cut squash in half lengthwise. Combine the apple pie filling and sugar and spoon into squash. Place sausage links in apple mixture and bake for 15 minutes longer or until squash is tender.

Autumn Dinner (above)

SAUSAGE-EGGPLANT CASSEROLE

1 med. eggplant	3 finely chopped green onions
2 med. tomatoes	and tops
1 tsp. oregano	1 egg
Pepper to taste	1 tbsp. milk
Seasoned salt to taste	1 lb. smoked sausage
2 tbsp. cracker meal	Buttered cracker crumbs
3/4 c. cubed Cheddar cheese	

Peel the eggplant and tomatoes and chop. Place in a saucepan and cook in small amount of salted water until soft. Add the oregano, pepper, seasoned salt, cracker meal, onions and cheese and mix well. Beat the egg with milk and stir into the eggplant mixture. Chop the sausage and cook in a skillet over low heat until done. Stir into the eggplant mixture. Place in a casserole and cover with cracker crumbs. Bake at 350 degrees for 25 minutes.

Mrs. Cecil V. Chapman, Lafayette, Louisiana

ELLENBURGER SPECIAL

2 lb. bulk sausage	1/3 c. chopped green pepper
3 pkg. chicken-noodle soup mix	1 sm. onion, chopped
6 c. boiling water	1 c. rice
2 c. chopped celery	1/2 c. chopped almonds or pecans

Brown the sausage in a skillet and drain off fat. Stir the soup mix into boiling water in a saucepan and bring to a boil. Simmer for 10 minutes. Add the sausage and remaining ingredients and mix well. Place in a casserole and refrigerate for 24 hours. Bake at 350 degrees for 1 hour.

Olive Parham, Shreveport, Louisiana

CHINESE ALMOND RICE

1 lb. bulk pork sausage	3 pkg. noodle soup mix
2 c. rice	9 c. boiling water
2 lge. onions, chopped	1/2 tsp. salt
2 celery stalks, chopped	1/2 tsp. pepper
1 bell pepper, chopped	1/2 lb. slivered almonds

Brown the sausage in a skillet and remove from skillet. Brown the rice in sausage grease in the skillet, stirring constantly. Add the onions, celery and bell pepper and cook for 15 minutes, stirring frequently. Add the sausage and place in a casserole. Stir the soup mix into the water in a saucepan and cook for 10 minutes. Add the salt and pepper and pour over rice mixture. Bake for 1 hour at 350 degrees. Sprinkle with almonds and bake for 30 minutes longer, adding water, if needed.

Florence Pribble, Ft. Worth, Texas

SPANISH SAUSAGE AND RICE

1 c. rice	1/2 tsp. paprika
1 pt. tomatoes	1/2 tsp. chili powder
1 pt. water	1/2 tsp. curry powder
1 Spanish onion, chopped	Salt to taste
1 lb. bulk pork sausage	

Combine all ingredients and mix well. Place in a casserole. Bake at 350 degrees for 1 hour.

Mrs. R. B. Hartzog, St. Matthew, South Carolina

SAUSAGE STEW

2 10 1/2-oz. cans beef bouillon	1 lge. green pepper, quartered
1/2 tsp. hot sauce	1 garlic clove
4 to 6 beef knockwurst, sliced	1/2 lb. pork sausage links
4 carrots, thinly sliced	Salt to taste
3 stalks celery, diced	

Heat the bouillon with hot sauce in a large saucepan. Add knockwurst, carrots, celery, green pepper and garlic clove and simmer for about 20 minutes. Cook the sausage links until brown and drain. Add to stew and simmer for about 10 minutes. Add salt. Serve with cooked, parslied potatoes. Frankfurters may be substituted for knockwurst. 4 servings.

Sausage Stew (above)

HAM AND BEAN RAGOUT

1 c. tomato soup	1 tsp. chili powder
2 c. cooked dried lima beans	2 c. chopped ham
1 10-oz. can cream-style corn	Salt and pepper to taste
1 bell pepper, chopped	

Mix the soup with 1 cup water in a large bowl. Add remaining ingredients and mix well. Place in a casserole and cover. Bake for 1 hour at 350 degrees.

Mrs. Harry Gremillion, Shreveport, Louisiana

OLD-FASHIONED HAM AND BEAN SOUP

1 lb. dried kidney beans	1/2 c. chopped carrots
3 qt. water	4 whole cloves
1 hambone with meat	1 bay leaf
1/2 c. chopped onion	1 tsp. salt
1/2 c. chopped celery	1/4 tsp. pepper

Place the beans and water in a large kettle and bring to a boil. Remove from heat, cover and let stand for 1 hour. Add the hambone, onion, celery, carrots, cloves, bay leaf, salt and pepper and simmer for 2 hours or until beans are tender. Remove hambone from soup, cut off meat and place in soup. Remove bay leaf. Garnish the servings with sieved hard-cooked egg yolk, if desired. 10-12 servings.

Sue Akers, Haleyville, Alabama

PORK RAGOUT

2 lb. pork	Grated rind of 1 lemon
1 1/2 c. chopped onions	1 clove of garlic
3/4 c. butter	1 tbsp. paprika
1 tsp. caraway seed	1 c. water or stock
2 tsp. marjoram	

Cut the pork into 1 1/2-inch cubes. Saute the onions in the butter in a saucepan. Mash the caraway seeds, marjoram, lemon rind, garlic and paprika in a mortar and add to onions. Stir in water and pork and bring to a boil. Simmer, covered, for 1 hour and 30 minutes. Garnish with strips of red or green peppers.

Gilbert Huffman, New Castle, Virginia

SPICY PORK CREOLE

2 lb. boneless pork shoulder	1/8 tsp. pepper
2 tbsp. butter or margarine	1/8 tsp. garlic powder
1/2 c. minced celery	1 can chicken broth
1/3 c. minced green pepper	1/4 c. bottled barbecue sauce
1 sm. onion, minced	3 tbsp. molasses

1 med. tomato	2 tbsp. cornstarch
1 tsp. salt	1/4 c. water

Cut the pork into 1/4-inch thick slices. Melt the butter in large skillet and brown pork well. Add the celery, green pepper and onion and cook until lightly browned. Peel the tomato, dice and add to pork mixture. Add the salt, pepper, garlic powder, broth, barbecue sauce and molasses. Simmer, covered, for 25 to 30 minutes or until pork is tender. Blend the cornstarch with water to a smooth paste and stir into pork mixture. Cook, stirring constantly, until thickened and clear. 4-5 servings.

Mrs. Flora Grissom, Jackson, Tennessee

CHEF'S FRUIT-HAM SALAD

1 1/2 c. mayonnaise	1 1/2 c. cantaloupe balls
1/4 c. pineapple juice	1 1/2 c. pineapple chunks
1 tbsp. lemon juice	1 c. seedless raisins
1 tsp. grated lemon peel	1 tbsp. melted butter
1/2 tsp. celery seed	1/2 tsp. cinnamon
Dash of hot sauce	1 1/2 c. thin strips cooked ham
1 qt. shredded crisp salad greens	or turkey
1 1/2 c. sliced bananas	1 1/2 c. thin strips Swiss cheese
1 1/2 c. halved strawberries	

Blend mayonnaise, pineapple juice, lemon juice, lemon peel, celery seed and hot sauce in a bowl. Cover and refrigerate for 1 hour or longer to blend flavors. Place the salad greens in a chilled serving bowl and arrange the fruits on top. Spoon small amount of dressing over all. Combine the raisins, melted butter and cinnamon in a saucepan and cook over low heat, stirring, for about 5 minutes. Cool. Place the ham strips, cheese strips and raisins at intervals over the fruit mixture and serve with remaining dressing. 6 servings.

Chef's Fruit-Ham Salad (above)

KIDNEY BEAN SALAD

1 can kidney beans, drained
1/2 c. chopped celery
1/2 c. diced green pepper
1 onion, cut in rings
1/2 c. chopped pickles

1/2 lb. cheese, grated
1 lb. ham, cut in strips
2 hard-cooked eggs, sliced
Mayonnaise

Combine all ingredients except mayonnaise and toss lightly. Chill. Add enough mayonnaise to moisten and mix lightly. Serve in lettuce cups.

Mrs. Mary Ann Lea, Vilonia, Arkansas

PATIO SALAD

1 c. cubed cooked pork
4 hard-cooked eggs, chopped
1/2 c. diced celery

1/2 c. diced sweet or sour pickle
Mayonnaise
Lettuce

Combine the pork, eggs, celery, and pickles in a bowl. Add enough mayonnaise to moisten and mix well. Serve in lettuce cups and garnish with paprika.

Mrs. Stella Forrest, Wake Forest, North Carolina

PORK ENSALADA

3/4 c. oil
1/8 c. cider vinegar
4 tbsp. lemon juice
1 clove of garlic
1/2 tsp. soy sauce
1 tsp. salt
Dash of cayenne pepper
1/2 tsp. curry powder
2 crushed juniper berries

2 c. diced lean roast pork
2 tbsp. unflavored gelatin
1 1/2 c. chicken broth
1/2 c. celery crescents
1/2 c. sliced cucumbers
1/2 c. grated carrots
2 tbsp. grated onion
Lettuce

Mix the oil, vinegar, 2 tablespoons lemon juice, garlic, soy sauce, salt, cayenne pepper, curry powder and juniper berries in a bowl. Add the pork and refrigerate for at least 4 hours or overnight, stirring occasionally. Soften the gelatin in 1/2 cup chicken broth. Heat remaining broth and dissolve gelatin in hot broth. Add remaining lemon juice and chill until partially set. Drain the pork and add to the gelatin mixture. Add the celery, cucumbers, carrots and onion and mix well. Pour into an oiled mold and chill until firm. Unmold on lettuce.

Mrs. J. L. Dixson, St. Petersburg, Florida

PORK AND APPLE SALAD

2 c. diced cooked pork
2 c. diced unpeeled red apples
1 c. diced celery
1/4 c. sweet relish

1 tbsp. lemon juice
1/4 tsp. onion juice
Dash of salt
1/3 c. mayonnaise

Combine all ingredients in a bowl and chill. Serve on lettuce. 4 servings.

Mrs. W. C. Dobbs, Arlington, Virginia

DANISH GARDEN SALAD

5 10-oz. packages frozen	1/4 tsp. pepper
Brussels sprouts	1 tsp. basil
8 env. unflavored gelatin	1/2 c. cooked sliced carrots
1 1/2 c. cold water	2 c. cooked sliced zucchini
5 1/2 c. hot chicken stock	2 c. cooked lima beans
1 c. bleu cheese	3 c. cooked ham strips
4 c. sour cream	

Cook the Brussels sprouts according to package directions, then drain and chill. Soften 6 envelopes gelatin in 1 cup water in a saucepan. Add 3 1/2 cups stock and cook over low heat, stirring constantly, until gelatin is dissolved. Chill until thickened. Mix the bleu cheese and sour cream until smooth and fold into gelatin. Add seasonings, carrots, zucchini and lima beans. Reserve 15 whole Brussels sprouts for garnish. Cut remaining Brussels sprouts in half and add to gelatin mixture. Turn into a lightly greased 15 x 4 1/2 x 4-inch loaf pan and chill until firm. Soften remaining gelatin in 1/2 cup water in a saucepan. Add remaining stock and cook over low heat, stirring constantly, until gelatin is dissolved. Chill until thickened. Arrange ham over congealed mold to cover top completely. Spoon gelatin over ham and chill until firm. Unmold onto chilled serving platter and garnish with reserved Brussels sprouts. May garnish with piped softened cream cheese, slices of hard-cooked egg, sliced truffles or rolled anchovy fillets, if desired.

Bleu Cheese Dressing

2 c. sour cream	1 c. bleu cheese
2 tsp. anchovy paste	1 tbsp. tarragon vinegar

Blend all ingredients in a bowl until smooth, then chill. Serve with salad.

Danish Garden Salad (above)

lamb & mutton

Lamb and mutton are to cooking what crushed velvet cloth is to sewing. Lamb and mutton, like velvet, have wonderfully smooth textures and produce lavishly beautiful products when prepared with care.

Because lamb and mutton dishes are so pleasing to the eye, they are ideal to serve at parties and on occasions when you want your table to look very special.

In addition to their visual beauty, these meats are deliciously different in taste. And lamb and mutton are easily prepared in numerous ways.

Try them as a meat curry, as a barbecue entree, or as an ideal main course to serve with your favorite sweet sauce. Or, you might want to use lamb and mutton for such standard favorites as roasts or chops.

Because lamb and mutton are generally more economical than beef, they are ideal for todays cost-conscious homemaker. The following variety of Southern recipes offers an exciting, economical cooking adventure.

At your most elegant party or at your family dinner table, lamb or mutton can add variety to your menu. And the visual appeal of this beautiful meat will make you proud to serve it often.

On the following pages, Southern homemakers share with you their favorite recipes for lamb and mutton. Each will add a new elegance to your table.

The delicate flavor of lamb brings delicious variety to family and company meals. In parts of the country where lamb is popular, it is sold all year. In other sections it is available only when the supply is plentiful — in the early fall and spring.

High-quality lamb has a smooth covering of clear white, brittle fat over most of the outside. The meat is pinkish-red, deepening to a darker red in older animals. It is always finely-grained and velvety-looking. Lamb is quality-stamped by government inspectors, using categories identical to those which classify beef (pp. 10-11).

The thin paper-like covering over lamb roasts and chops is called the "fell." Chops will taste and look better if this is removed. The fell should not be

general directions
FOR LAMB

removed from roasts — it helps the roast keep its shape, cook in less time, and stay juicy. Lamb's mild flavor can be enhanced by careful use of a few herbs. Particularly good with lamb chops and roasts are rosemary, thyme, and mint.

Because most cuts of high-quality lamb are tender, they can be cooked by dry heat methods — roasting, broiling, pan-broiling. The neck, shanks, and breasts may be braised or cut into small pieces and stewed. The meat from these cuts is also ground for patties or loaves. Lamb is always cooked medium or well done. If it is cooked so that it is still slightly pink on the inside, there will be less shrinkage and the meat will be deliciously juicy.

Lamb roasts may be seasoned or not, as taste dictates. They should always be served either piping hot on a heated platter or icy cold, never lukewarm. The serving platter may be garnished with parsley, mint, or other herbs.

Lamb chops are especially delicious if marinated before broiling. Try a mixture of salad oil, lemon juice, salt, and cut garlic cloves. In other marinades, substitute thyme or a bay leaf and paprika in place of the garlic. For an especially unusual flavor, try salad oil, catsup, chopped onion, curry powder, and a dash of hot pepper sauce. English-style broiled chops are a special favorite with men. Cut two 1-inch thick chops from an unsplit loin. Remove the rib bones. Insert a lamb kidney between the two chops and hold it in place by wrapping the flank ends of the chop around the kidney. Fasten with a skewer and broil as for chops, about 15 minutes on each side or until medium well-done.

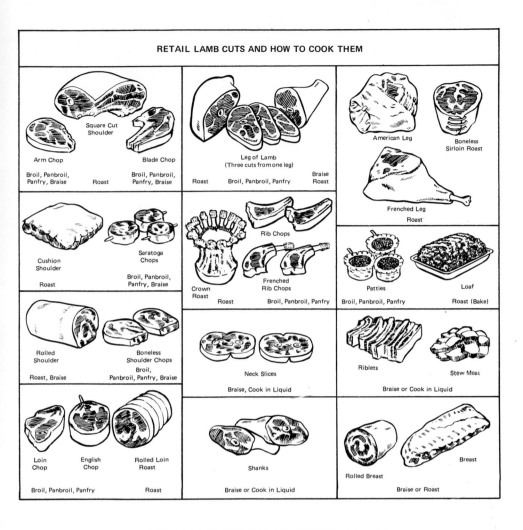

RETAIL LAMB CUTS AND HOW TO COOK THEM

Square Cut Shoulder

Arm Chop
Broil, Panbroil, Panfry, Braise

Blade Chop
Broil, Panbroil, Panfry, Braise

Roast

Leg of Lamb
(Three cuts from one leg)
Roast   Broil, Panbroil, Panfry

Braise
Roast

American Leg

Boneless
Sirloin Roast

Frenched Leg
Roast

Cushion Shoulder
Roast

Saratoga Chops
Broil, Panbroil, Panfry, Braise

Rib Chops

Crown Roast
Roast

Frenched Rib Chops
Broil, Panbroil, Panfry

Patties
Broil, Panbroil, Panfry

Loaf
Roast (Bake)

Rolled Shoulder
Roast, Braise

Boneless Shoulder Chops
Broil, Panbroil, Panfry, Braise

Neck Slices
Braise, Cook in Liquid

Riblets

Stew Meat

Braise or Cook in Liquid

Loin Chop

English Chop

Rolled Loin Roast

Broil, Panbroil, Panfry   Roast

Shanks
Braise or Cook in Liquid

Rolled Breast
Braise or Roast

Breast

TIMETABLE FOR COOKING LAMB

| CUT | ROASTED AT 300 F. OVEN TEMPERATURE | | BROILED | BRAISED | COOKED IN LIQUID |
	Meat Thermometer Reading Degrees F.	Time Minutes per lb.	Time Minutes	Total Time Hours	Time Hours
Leg	175 to 180	30 to 35			
Shoulder (Whole)	175 to 180	30 to 35			
Rolled	175 to 180	40 to 45			
Cushion	175 to 180	30 to 35			
Breast (Stuffed)				1 1/2 to 2	
Rolled	175 to 180	30 to 35		1 1/2 to 2	
Lamb Loaf	175 to 180	30 to 35			
Chops (1 inch)	175 to 180	30 to 35	12		
Chops (1 1/2 inch)			18		
Chops (2 inch)			22		
Lamb Patties (1 inch)			15 to 18		
Neck Slices				1	
Shanks				1 1/2	
Stew					1 1/2 to 2
Panbroiling requires approximately one-half the time of broiling.					

SHAKER LAMB DINNER

1 leg of lamb	1/4 tsp. crushed rosemary leaves
Salt and pepper to taste	Mushroom Sauce
Flour	Mashed or baked potatoes
1/4 c. butter	

Score fat on top of lamb. Sprinkle lamb with salt and pepper and rub with flour. Place on rack in a shallow roasting pan. Roast in 325-degree oven for 30 to 35 minutes per pound or until meat thermometer registers 175 degrees for medium doneness. Melt the butter in a saucepan and stir in the rosemary. Brush on lamb during last 2 hours of roasting time. Serve lamb with Mushroom Sauce and potatoes.

Mushroom Sauce

1/2 lb. mushrooms, sliced	1/8 tsp. pepper
1 sm. onion, chopped	2 c. milk
1/4 tsp. crushed rosemary leaves	1/2 c. light cream
1/4 c. butter	1/2 c. toasted sliced almonds
3 tbsp. flour	2 tbsp. chopped parsley
1 tsp. salt	

Saute the mushrooms, onion and rosemary in butter until lightly browned, then mix in flour, salt and pepper. Add milk gradually and cook, stirring constantly, until sauce boils for 1 minute. Add the cream and cook over low heat until thickened. Sprinkle almonds and parsley over the top.

Photograph for this recipe on page 98.

LAMB BASILÉ

Leg of lamb	Crumbled basil to taste
Bacon, cut in cubes	1 lge. bay leaf
Garlic slivers	1 c. orange juice
Salt and pepper to taste	3 tbsp. Triple Sec
Finely chopped celery to taste	4 slices bacon

Preheat oven to 300 degrees. Make small cuts at 1-inch intervals over the leg of lamb with small paring knife. Stick bacon cubes and garlic in cuts and rub lamb with salt and pepper. Place the leg of lamb on a rack in a Dutch oven. Mix the celery, basil and bay leaf with orange juice and add Triple Sec. Pour mixture slowly over leg of lamb. Place bacon slices across top of lamb and cover Dutch oven. Roast for 40 minutes per pound, basting every 15 minutes. Uncover Dutch oven and bake for 15 minutes longer or until brown. Serve hot or cold garnished with mint.

Mrs. Glenn Ward Dresbach, Eureka Springs, Arkansas

PIQUANT LEG OF LAMB

1 tsp. salt	1/2 tsp. pepper
1/2 tsp. monosodium glutamate	1 tsp. seasoned salt

1/2 tsp. ground marjoram
1/4 tsp. dry mustard
1/8 tsp. ground cardamom
1 6-lb. leg of lamb

2 cloves of garlic, slivered
1/2 tsp. ground thyme
Slivered orange peel

Mix the salt, monosodium glutamate, pepper, seasoned salt, marjoram, mustard and cardamom and rub on the leg of lamb. Toss garlic and thyme together. Cut 16 deep slits in the lamb and insert garlic and orange peel into each slit. Place the lamb, fat side up, on a rack in a shallow roasting pan and insert meat thermometer into center of thickest part. Roast at 325 degrees for about 3 hours or until the meat thermometer registers 175 degrees for medium done or 180 degrees for well done. Garnish with sprigs of mint. 10 servings.

Mrs. Andrew Johnson, Green Mountain, North Carolina

BUCKINGHAM GLAZED LEG OF LAMB

1 leg of lamb
Salt and pepper to taste
1/2 c. dry sherry
1/2 c. currant jelly

1/2 c. catsup
1/2 tsp. marjoram leaves
Parsley
Lemon wedges

Sprinkle the lamb with salt and pepper and place on rack in a shallow roasting pan. Roast in 325-degree oven for 30 to 35 minutes per pound or until meat thermometer registers 175 degrees for medium doneness. Combine the sherry, jelly, catsup and marjoram in a small saucepan and heat, stirring, until jelly melts. Brush on lamb occasionally during last 1 hour and 30 minutes of roasting time. Heat remaining sauce and serve with lamb. Garnish with parsley and lemon wedges.

Buckingham Glazed Leg of Lamb (above)

LEG OF LAMB

1 stick butter or margarine	Garlic salt to taste
Juice of 3 lemons	3 bay leaves
Worcestershire sauce to taste	Leg of lamb
Dry mustard to taste	Salt to taste
Monosodium glutamate	Chopped parsley
3 tbsp. olive or cooking oil	Paprika
Cracked pepper to taste	

Combine the butter, lemon juice, Worcestershire sauce, mustard, desired amount of monosodium glutamate, olive oil, pepper, garlic salt and bay leaves in a saucepan and bring to a boil. Remove from heat and cool. Place the leg of lamb in a Dutch oven and sprinkle with salt. Pour the butter mixture over lamb and marinate in refrigerator for 12 to 24 hours. Cover the Dutch oven. Roast at 450 degrees for 1 hour and 30 minutes. Decrease temperature to 350 degrees and roast until done. Sprinkle with parsley, paprika and additional cracked pepper.

Claud W. Dodd, Durant, Mississippi

ROAST LEG OF LAMB NORMANDE

1 3-lb. leg of lamb	1 vegetable bouillon cube
1/2 tsp. pepper	1/2 c. hot water
1 tsp. salt	2 tbsp. applejack or bourbon
1/4 c. butter	1 c. heavy cream
2 tbsp. flour	

Sprinkle the leg of lamb with pepper and salt. Melt the butter in a shallow roasting pan and place lamb in butter. Roast at 375 degrees for 1 hour and 40 minutes, turning lamb frequently and basting with pan juices. Place lamb on a shallow ovenproof platter and keep warm. Drain all except 3 tablespoons drippings from pan. Add flour and mix well. Cook over low heat for 5 minutes. Mix the bouillon cube with hot water until dissolved and stir into flour mixture. Stir in the applejack and bring to a boil, scraping bottom of pan. Cook for 3 minutes longer. Add cream and stir well. Cover and simmer for 3 minutes longer. Serve with lamb. 6 servings.

Ramona Beachum, Peachland, North Carolina

LEG OF LAMB WITH MINT MERINGUE PEACHES

1 5 to 6-lb. leg of lamb	1/2 c. mint jelly
Salt and pepper to taste	8 to 10 peach halves
2 egg whites	

Season the leg of lamb with salt and pepper and place, skin side down, on a rack in a roasting pan. Insert a meat thermometer so the bulb reaches center of the thickest part of lamb, being sure the bulb does not rest in fat or on bone. Roast, uncovered, at 300 degrees for 2 hours and 30 minutes to 3 hours or to desired doneness. Do not add water. Beat the egg whites until stiff. Add the mint jelly gradually and continue beating until well mixed. Place a large spoon of mint meringue in each peach half and place peaches in shallow baking dish. Broil until the meringue is lightly browned and serve hot with the lamb.

Mrs. W. W. Smith, Alton, Virginia

PENINSULA LAMB SHANKS

6 1-lb. lamb shanks	1 med. onion, sliced
1 1/2 tsp. salt	2 cloves of garlic, finely minced
1/4 tsp. ground pepper	4 c. sliced celery
3 tbsp. oil	3 med. tomatoes, cut into wedges
3 tbsp. flour	1 tbsp. chopped parsley
1 10 1/2-oz. can chicken broth	

Sprinkle the lamb shanks with salt and pepper. Heat the oil in a Dutch oven. Add lamb shanks and brown well on all sides. Remove lamb shanks and set aside. Drain all but 2 tablespoons oil from Dutch oven. Stir flour into oil and brown lightly. Blend in broth and 1 3/4 cups water gradually and bring to boiling point. Return lamb shanks to Dutch oven and add the onion and garlic. Reduce heat and cover. Simmer for 1 hour and 30 minutes or until lamb is tender. Remove lamb to a warm serving platter. Add the celery to liquid in Dutch oven and cook for 10 minutes. Add the tomatoes and parsley and cook for 5 minutes longer. Spoon over lamb shanks. Serve with rice or mashed potatoes, if desired. 6 servings.

Peninsula Lamb Shanks (above)

LAMB CHOPS CALIFORNIA STYLE

6 lamb shoulder chops, 1 in. thick	1 1/2 tsp. salt
1 tbsp. salad oil	1 tsp. monosodium glutamate
1/4 c. sliced onion	1/2 tsp. ginger
2 1-lb. 14-oz. cans yellow cling peach halves	1/4 tsp. dry mustard
1 tsp. grated lime peel	1 3-in. cinnamon stick
1/4 c. lime juice	1 tbsp. cornstarch
1 tbsp. honey	12 to 16 whole strawberries

Brown the lamb chops in oil in a large skillet. Remove the chops and drain off all but 1/2 tablespoon drippings. Add the onion to drippings and saute until tender.

Add the chops. Drain the peaches and reserve syrup. Mix 3/4 cup reserved peach syrup, lime peel, lime juice, honey, salt, monosodium glutamate, ginger, mustard and cinnamon stick and pour over chops. Simmer, covered, for 40 to 45 minutes or until chops are fork-tender. Remove the lamb chops to a serving dish and keep hot. Blend the cornstarch with 1 tablespoon reserved peach syrup. Stir into simmering sauce in skillet and cook for 30 seconds, stirring constantly. Add peaches, cut side up, and top each peach half with a strawberry. Cover and heat for 2 to 5 minutes or until heated through. Remove peaches to serving dish with lamb and pour sauce over all. Garnish with watercress. 6 servings.

BROILED LAMB CHOPS

4 loin lamb chops, cut 1 1/2 in. thick	Dash of pepper
1 tsp. salt	4 slices pineapple

Preheat oven to 350 degrees. Sprinkle the lamb chops with salt and pepper. Place the pineapple slices on rack of a broiler pan and place the lamb chops on pineapple. Broil 2 inches from heat until the lamb chops are well browned.

Martha A. Avery, Bells, Tennessee

LAMB CHOPS WITH SPINACH DRESSING

1 med. onion, minced	4 1/2 c. chopped fresh spinach
1 tbsp. fat	4 1/2 c. fine soft bread crumbs
6 shoulder lamb chops	2 eggs
2 tsp. salt	Celery salt to taste

Saute the onion in fat in a skillet until soft, remove from skillet and set aside. Season the lamb chops with 1/2 teaspoon salt and brown in the skillet on both sides over low heat. Combine the spinach, bread crumbs, onion, eggs, remaining salt and celery salt and blend well. Place the spinach dressing in a shallow baking dish and top with the lamb chops. Bake, covered, at 350 degrees for 1 hour or until the chops are tender.

Mrs. William B. Marks, Harrisonburg, Virginia

BROILED LAMB CHOPS WITH ONION SAUCE

4 loin lamb chops, 1 in. thick	3/4 c. white wine
1 1/2 c. chopped onions	1 tsp. salt
1/4 c. butter or margarine	1/3 c. chopped parsley

Place the lamb chops on rack in a broiler pan. Broil 3 to 4 inches from heat for 5 to 7 minutes on each side or to desired doneness. Saute the onions in butter in a saucepan until golden. Add the wine and salt and bring to a boil. Reduce heat and simmer for 5 minutes. Add parsley and serve over lamb chops. 4 servings.

Photograph for this recipe on page 4.

LAMB PATTIES

1 lb. ground lamb	1/4 c. milk
Dash of monosodium glutamate	Peach halves
Dash of marjoram	Mint jelly
1 tsp. salt	Bacon strips

Combine the lamb, monosodium glutamate, marjoram, salt and milk in a mixing bowl and mix well. Shape into 4 oval patties and score with a spatula. Place the patties and peach halves on a broiler pan. Broil about 4 or 5 inches from heat for 12 minutes. Turn patties and broil for 5 minutes. Fill each peach half with mint jelly and top each patty with a strip of bacon. Broil for 5 minutes longer.

Mrs. Albert Norvell, Wewoka, Oklahoma

LAMB LOAF WITH CHILI HOLLANDAISE

1 1/2 lb. ground lamb	1 1/4 tsp. salt
1/3 c. milk	1/4 tsp. pepper
1/2 c. fine cracker crumbs	1/4 c. chili sauce
1 med. onion, chopped	1 6-oz. jar hollandaise sauce

Combine the lamb, milk, crumbs, onion, salt and pepper in a bowl and mix well. Press into a 9 x 5 x 3-inch loaf pan. Bake at 350 degrees for 1 hour or until done. Combine the chili sauce and hollandaise sauce in a saucepan and cook over low heat until heated through. Serve with lamb loaf. 6 servings.

Lavada Stansberry, Whitney, Texas

LAMB LOAF

2 lb. ground lamb	1/8 tsp. poultry seasoning
1 c. bread crumbs	Salt and pepper to taste
1 onion, finely minced	1 egg, lightly beaten
1/2 green pepper, finely minced	1 c. meat stock or milk

Combine the lamb, bread crumbs, onion, green pepper and seasonings in a mixing bowl. Add the egg and meat stock and mix well. Pack into a ring mold. Bake at 350 degrees for about 1 hour and 30 minutes or until done. Unmold and fill center with parsley-buttered potato balls.

Mrs. Annie Elliott, Belcross, North Carolina

GROUND LAMB CASSEROLE

1 lb. ground lamb	1 c. fine dry bread crumbs
1/4 lb. chopped mushrooms	1 tsp. salt
1/2 c. finely chopped green pepper	1/4 tsp. pepper
1 med. onion, finely chopped	1 c. chili sauce

Cook the lamb in a skillet over low heat, stirring occasionally, until browned and drain off drippings. Add the remaining ingredients and mix well. Turn into a 1-quart casserole. Bake at 350 degrees for 1 hour. 4 servings.

Mrs. Guy Hogan, Atlanta, Georgia

PERSIAN LAMB WITH RHUBARB SAUCE

2 1/2 c. cut fresh rhubarb	1/4 to 1/2 tsp. pepper
3/4 c. sugar	1/2 tsp. ground cinnamon
1 lb. lamb	1/4 tsp. ground nutmeg
1/4 c. butter	1 c. chopped parsley
1 lge. onion, chopped	1 tbsp. cornstarch
1 tsp. salt	2 c. hot cooked rice

Place the rhubarb in a bowl and stir in sugar and 3/4 cup water. Let set for 30 minutes, then drain, reserving syrup. Cut the lamb into 1-inch pieces. Melt butter in a 10-inch skillet and saute lamb, onion, salt, pepper, cinnamon and nutmeg until lamb is browned. Stir in the parsley and saute for several minutes longer. Stir in reserved rhubarb syrup and cover. Simmer for 40 minutes. Stir in the rhubarb and cover. Simmer for 20 to 30 minutes or until lamb is tender. Mix the cornstarch and 1 tablespoon water and stir into lamb mixture. Cook over low heat for 2 to 3 minutes longer or until thickened. Serve over rice. One 1-pound can colored rhubarb may be substituted for fresh rhubarb, decreasing water to 1/2 cup and omitting sugar. 4 servings.

Persian Lamb with Rhubarb Sauce (above)

LAMB BARBECUE AND NOODLES

1 sm. onion, sliced	1/4 c. water
2 tbsp. butter or margarine	1 tsp. Worcestershire sauce
1 to 2 tbsp. vinegar	1 c. chopped cooked roast lamb
2 tsp. brown sugar	1 1/2 c. medium noodles
1/2 c. catsup	

Saute the onion in 1 tablespoon butter in a small saucepan until lightly browned. Add the vinegar, brown sugar, catsup, water and Worcestershire sauce and bring to a boil. Simmer, covered, for 15 minutes. Add the lamb and simmer until heated through. Cook the noodles according to package directions and drain. Add remaining butter and place in a serving dish. Pour the lamb mixture over the noodles. 2 servings.

Edna Mae Basden, Rienzi, Mississippi

LAMB CURRY

1 1/2 tbsp. flour	1 tbsp. sugar
1 tsp. salt	2 med. onions, chopped
1/2 tsp. garlic salt	2 med. apples, diced
1 1/2 lb. lamb, cut in cubes	3/4 c. hot water
2 tbsp. butter	Hot buttered rice
1 tbsp. curry powder	Paprika

Combine the flour, salt and garlic salt and dredge the lamb with the flour mixture. Melt the butter in a large skillet. Add the curry powder, sugar, onions and apples and cook over low heat until onions are tender. Remove onion mixture from the skillet and set aside. Brown the lamb in remaining drippings in the skillet. Add the onion mixture and water and cover the skillet. Simmer for 1 hour. Arrange the rice on a heated serving platter and sprinkle with paprika. Pour the lamb mixture into center of rice. Serve with chutney, shredded coconut, peanuts and raisins in small dishes.

Mrs. Lodus Phillips, Baldwyn, Mississippi

CURRIED LAMB AND RICE

Flour	1/4 c. sliced onion
1 tsp. salt	2 tsp. curry powder
1/2 tsp. pepper	1 c. evaporated milk
2 lb. lean shoulder lamb, cubed	1 c. unpeeled chopped red apple
2 tbsp. butter	2 c. cooked rice
1 1/2 c. boiling water	2 tbsp. parsley flakes

Mix 1/4 cup flour, salt and pepper together and dredge lamb with flour mixture. Reserve remaining flour mixture. Melt the butter in a large frypan, add lamb and brown well on all sides. Add the boiling water and onion and cover. Cook over low heat for 1 to 2 hours or until the lamb is tender. Measure reserved flour and add enough flour to make 1/4 cup. Add the curry powder and mix well. Stir into lamb mixture and blend well. Add the milk slowly and cook over low heat, stirring constantly, for about 5 minutes or until thickened. Stir in the apple just before serving. Serve over the rice and garnish with parsley.

Mrs. Ezra Bailey, Lancaster, South Carolina

SHISH KABOB WITH RICE PILAF

1/4 c. tarragon vinegar	1 green pepper
1/2 c. dry white wine	2 firm tomatoes, quartered
2 tbsp. salad oil	8 med. mushrooms
1 clove of garlic, minced	1/4 c. butter
2 tbsp. mixed pickling spice	1 c. rice
1/4 tsp. crushed rosemary	2 tbsp. minced onion
2 lb. boned lamb shoulder	2 c. chicken broth

Combine the vinegar, wine, oil, garlic, pickling spice and rosemary and mix well. Cut the lamb in 1 1/2-inch cubes and place in a bowl. Pour the vinegar mixture over lamb and marinate in refrigerator for several hours or overnight. Drain the lamb and reserve marinade. Cut the green pepper in 1 1/2-inch squares. Alternate cubes of lamb, green pepper, tomato and mushrooms on 4 large skewers and brush with reserved marinade. Place on rack in a broiler pan. Broil 3 to 4 inches from heat for 8 to 10 minutes on each side. Melt the butter in a saucepan and add rice and onion. Cook, stirring constantly, until rice is lightly browned. Add the chicken broth and cover saucepan. Simmer for 20 to 25 minutes or until all liquid is absorbed and rice is tender. Place in a serving dish and place kabobs on the rice. 4 servings.

Shish Kabob with Rice Pilaf (above)

RIBS OF MUTTON

2 lb. mutton ribs	1 tbsp. prepared mustard
Seasoned flour	2 c. water
3 tbsp. (about) peanut oil	

Cut the ribs into serving pieces and dredge with seasoned flour. Fry in the oil in Dutch oven until browned on both sides. Add the mustard and water and stir well. Cover Dutch oven. Simmer the ribs until tender, adding water as needed.

Mrs. Anne W. Herbert, Atlanta, Georgia

ITALIAN LAMB STEW

2 lb. lamb neck slices	1/8 tsp. pepper
2 tbsp. salad oil	1 bay leaf
1 sm. onion, sliced	2 med. zucchini
1 clove of garlic, minced	1/4 lb. small mushrooms
1 20-oz. can tomatoes	2 20-oz. cans white kidney beans
1 1/2 tsp. salt	1/2 c. small stuffed olives
1/4 tsp. oregano leaves	

Brown the lamb in oil in a large skillet. Remove lamb and discard drippings. Combine the onion, garlic, tomatoes, salt, oregano, pepper and bay leaf in the skillet. Add lamb and cover. Simmer for 45 minutes, then remove the bay leaf. Cut the zucchini in 1/2-inch slices and add to lamb mixture. Add the mushrooms and mix well. Cook for 15 minutes or until vegetables and lamb are tender. Drain the kidney beans and add to lamb mixture. Add the olives and cook for about 5 minutes longer.

Italian Lamb Stew (above)

ROCKY MOUNTAIN LAMB RIBLETS

1 12-oz. bottle hot catsup	1/4 tsp. celery seed
1/2 c. orange juice	1/4 tsp. rosemary leaves
1/4 c. chopped parsley	3 lb. lamb riblets

Combine the catsup, orange juice, parsley, celery seed and rosemary leaves. Cut the riblets into serving pieces and place in shallow, oblong dish. Pour the sauce over riblets and marinate in refrigerator overnight. Drain the riblets and reserve marinade. Brown riblets well in a large skillet. Arrange the riblets in a baking dish and add reserved marinade. Cover baking dish. Bake in 375-degree oven for 35 to 40 minutes or until tender. 4 servings.

Jean Delancey, Colt, Arkansas

SWEET-SOUR LAMB RIBLETS

4 lb. lamb riblets	1/4 c. vinegar
1/2 c. soy sauce	1/2 c. chopped candied ginger
2 to 3 c. brown sugar	2 tbsp. catsup
1/2 c. water	1 tbsp. cornstarch

Separate the riblets into serving pieces and remove excess fat. Arrange in shallow roasting pan. Bake in 400-degree oven for about 30 minutes or until brown, turning occasionally and pouring off accumulated fat. Combine the soy sauce, sugar, water, vinegar, ginger, catsup and cornstarch in a bowl and mix well. Pour over the riblets and cover pan. Bake at 325 degrees for 1 hour to 1 hour and 30 minutes, turning riblets occasionally and basting with sauce. Add a small amount of water if sauce becomes too thick.

Ann Elsie Schmetzer, Madisonville, Kentucky

MT. EVEREST HOT STEW

3 lb. lamb	1 1/2 c. boiling water
2 tbsp. salad oil	1 tsp. pepper sauce
4 lge. carrots, cubed	1 tsp. salt
4 lge. onions, cubed	8 whole cloves
8 lge. potatoes, cubed	2 tbsp. flour

Cut the lamb into cubes and brown in the salad oil in a heavy skillet. Add the carrots, onions, potatoes, water, pepper sauce and salt. Tie the cloves in cheesecloth and add to the lamb mixture. Cover the skillet and simmer lamb for 2 hours. Drain and measure the liquid. Mix 1 tablespoon flour and 1 tablespoon water together for each cup of liquid. Blend well, add to liquid and cook slowly, stirring constantly, until thickened. Add the thickened sauce to the lamb.
PERSONAL NOTE: High in the Himalayas lies Mt. Everest Hotel. After the long walking tour of Upper Town and Lower Town in below freezing weather, and the difficult climb back to the hotel, this stew is not to be forgotten.

Flora Chambers, Wauchula, Florida

LAMB SOUP JULIENNE

2 carrots	1 stick butter
2 med. potatoes	1 4-oz. can green peas
2 sm. onions	Salt and pepper to taste
4 cabbage leaves	1 1/2 qt. water
1 med. turnip	1 lb. lamb, cut in cubes

Cut the first 5 vegetables into thin strips. Melt the butter in a large saucepan and saute the cut vegetables in butter for 4 minutes, stirring gently. Add the remaining ingredients and bring to boiling point. Reduce heat and simmer for 30 minutes or until lamb is done, adding water as needed. 4 servings.

Mrs. Remington McConnell, Atlanta, Georgia

SPICED MUTTON BOWL

2 lb. mutton, cut in cubes	Salt and pepper to taste
4 onions, chopped	2 tsp. paprika
1 1/2 pt. water	1 tbsp. chopped parsley
1 c. vinegar	

Place the mutton and onions in a large saucepan and add the water, vinegar, salt, pepper and paprika. Bring to a boil and simmer for 1 hour and 30 minutes to 2 hours or until the mutton is tender. Serve very hot with chopped parsley sprinkled over the top. May serve with dumplings or potato balls if desired. 6 servings.

Mrs. Carrol McConnell, Montgomery, Alabama

MUTTON RAGOUT

2 lb. neck of mutton	Salt and pepper to taste
1/2 lb. onions	1 pt. stock or water
2 lb. potatoes	Chopped parsley

Cut the mutton into cutlets and trim, removing as much fat as possible. Place the mutton in a large saucepan. Peel the onions and slice into rings. Peel the potatoes and slice. Place onions and half the potatoes over the mutton and add salt and pepper. Pour the stock over mutton mixture and simmer gently for about 1 hour and 30 minutes. Place the remaining potatoes on top and simmer for 40 minutes longer. Place the mutton on a serving platter and place potatoes and onions around the mutton. Pour the liquid over all and garnish with the parsley.

Mrs. Terry Walls, Prattville, Alabama

HOT LAMB SALAD

1/2 head lettuce	1 onion, chopped
1 tomato, diced	1 lb. ground lamb

1 8-oz. can tomato sauce	Salt and pepper to taste
1 tbsp. (about) chili powder	1 med. package corn chips

Combine the lettuce, tomato and onion in a large mixing bowl. Brown the lamb in a skillet, stirring frequently. Add the tomato sauce, chili powder, salt and pepper and cook until heated through. Pour the lamb mixture over lettuce mixture and toss. Add the corn chips and toss lightly. Serve immediately. 6 servings.

Mrs. Allen Daggett, Houston, Texas

LAMB-VEGETABLE SALAD

1 c. sour cream	1 10-oz. package frozen green peas
1 tbsp. chopped chives	3 c. cubed cooked lamb
1 tsp. salt	3/4 c. coarsely grated carrots
1/4 tsp. seasoned pepper	Romaine
1 tbsp. lemon juice	Tomato wedges

Blend the sour cream with chives, salt, pepper and lemon juice in a bowl and chill. Cook the peas according to package directions, then drain and cool. Mix with the lamb and carrots and chill. Turn into romaine-lined bowl and garnish with tomato wedges. Toss with dressing just before serving. 6 servings.

Lamb-Vegetable Salad (above)

Spaghetti with Veal and Peppers (page 127)

veal

What is "veal" and how is it used by homemakers as tempting meat entrees? While veal has many uses, most cooks think of it as available only in cutlet form.

Veal, the flesh of a young calf, may be America's most misunderstood meat.

The following recipes attempt to bridge this gap by providing tasty dishes which use a wide variety of cuts of veal. Shared by Southern homemakers who are readers of *Southern Living,* these recipes can add a wealth of information to your cooking knowledge.

For instance, have you ever thought of using veal in a salad? One of the recipes will tell you how diced veal, when combined with vegetables and other ingredients, can become a nutritious and delicious salad entree.

Other recipes call for veal shank, leg, steak, chops, and roast. And you will also find exciting Southern recipes for the traditional veal cutlet.

Whatever your choice, the following recipes are good examples of the various uses for veal. By trying them, you will find this type of meat an appealing alternative in your never-ending search for food variety.

Veal — meat from young beef (calves) — is appetizing fare for family and company dining. Its flavor and texture are similar to those of chicken — delicate, juicy, and tender. Like chicken, veal combines well with many other flavors. That's one reason why it's such a favorite for spicy French and Italian-style recipes — its mild flavor is the perfect accompaniment to the tomatoes, herbs, spices, peppers, and other ingredients which are so much a part of these recipes.

Better grades of veal are graded similarly to beef — Prime, Choice, or Good. Some meat packers may use their own equivalent rating system, but most veal sold will be quality-rated.

Because veal comes from young animals, it has very little fat. In the best

general directions
FOR VEAL

meat, the fat is clear, firm, and white. The lean is pale pink and has no fat marbling. It is very fine, velvety-looking and firm — but not as firm as beef. Roasts or chops from older animals more readily resemble beef in flavor and texture.

Veal lacks fat. It contains a great deal of sinewy connective tissue. So it requires long, slow cooking to bring out both its tenderness and its delightfully delicate flavor. Such cooking methods as roasting, braising, frying, or stewing will make the flavor more pronounced.

If veal is roasted, it may be necessary to cover it with strips of salt pork or fat bacon. Veal chops, steaks, and cutlets are best when braised. Before cooking, they should be given a protective coating to minimize loss of natural juices. Try rolling them in a mixture of bread or cracker crumbs and some of the seasonings which are particularly good with veal — garlic, thyme, or parsley. For a flavor treat, before cooking let the veal marinate for a few minutes in a French dressing seasoned with either herbs or a dash of chili sauce.

Like all delicate meats, veal will pick up the flavor of the liquid in which it is cooked. For variety, try sweet or sour cream, cream of mushroom soup, chicken or celery soup, or any one of the many tart jellies or marmalades. Veal has so little natural fat that it will dry and lose flavor if it is broiled. But whatever the cooking method, it should always be cooked well-done.

Served on a heated platter, veal will stay hot and juicy for your family's dining pleasure.

RETAIL VEAL CUTS AND HOW TO COOK THEM

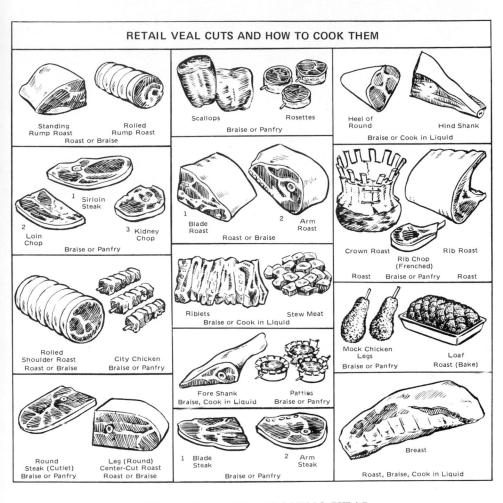

Standing Rump Roast   Rolled Rump Roast
Roast or Braise

Scallops   Rosettes
Braise or Panfry

Heel of Round   Hind Shank
Braise or Cook in Liquid

1 Sirloin Steak
2 Loin Chop
3 Kidney Chop
Braise or Panfry

1 Blade Roast
2 Arm Roast
Roast or Braise

Crown Roast   Rib Roast
Rib Chop (Frenched)
Roast   Braise or Panfry   Roast

Rolled Shoulder Roast
Roast or Braise
City Chicken
Braise or Panfry

Riblets   Stew Meat
Braise or Cook in Liquid

Mock Chicken Legs
Braise or Panfry
Loaf
Roast (Bake)

Fore Shank
Braise, Cook in Liquid
Patties
Braise or Panfry

Round Steak (Cutlet)
Braise or Panfry
Leg (Round) Center-Cut Roast
Roast or Braise

1 Blade Steak
2 Arm Steak
Braise or Panfry

Breast
Roast, Braise, Cook in Liquid

TIMETABLE FOR COOKING VEAL

CUT	ROASTED AT 300 F. OVEN TEMPERATURE		BRAISED	COOKED IN LIQUID
	Meat Thermometer Reading Degrees F.	Time Minutes per lb.	Total Time Hours	Total Time Hours
Leg	170	25		
Loin	170	30 to 35		
Rack	170	30 to 35		
Shoulder (Whole)	170	25		
Rolled	170	40 to 45		
Cushion	170	30 to 35		
Breast (Stuffed)	170	40 to 45	1 1/2 to 2	
Rolled	170	40 to 45	1 1/2 to 2	
Loaf	170	25 to 30		
Birds			3/4 to 1	
Chops			3/4 to 1	
Steaks			3/4 to 1	
Stew				2 to 2 1/2

119

VEAL ROAST ITALIANO

1 5-lb. leg or rump veal roast	1 sweet green pepper
1 8-oz. package pepperoni	1 sweet red pepper
2 tsp. seasoned salt	Bottled Italian salad dressing

Bone the veal roast. Cut the pepperoni in 4 pieces and place in pocket of the veal. Tie the roast with string. Rub with seasoned salt and place on a rack in roasting pan. Roast in 325-degree oven for about 3 hours. Remove from oven and cool, then chill. Cut the green and red peppers into squares and place in a bowl. Pour boiling water over peppers to cover and let stand for 5 minutes. Drain and drizzle lightly with salad dressing. Carve the roast and place on a large platter. Garnish with seasoned pepper squares.

Tuna Sauce

1 7-oz. can tuna	2 anchovy fillets, chopped
1/2 c. chicken broth	2 tbsp. capers, well drained
1/4 c. whipping cream	1 tsp. chopped pimento
2 drops of red pepper seasoning	

Combine the tuna and chicken broth in a blender container and cover. Blend for several minutes or until thick and smooth. Add the cream and red pepper seasoning and blend for about 1 minute longer. Stir in the anchovies, capers and pimento and pour into a serving bowl. Chill until served. Sauce will keep for only 1 hour in refrigerator. Serve over Veal Roast Italiano. 12 servings.

Mrs. Emelea B. Velaseo, McAllen, Texas

STUFFED VEAL LOIN

1 4-lb. veal loin, boned	Grated rind of 1 lemon
3 tbsp. lemon juice	Salt and pepper to taste
3 anchovy fillets, mashed	1 egg yolk
1 lge. can chopped mushrooms	Milk
1/2 lb. bacon	1/2 c. melted butter
1 c. bread crumbs	2 c. beef stock
1/2 c. chopped parsley	

Remove skin from the veal and sprinkle veal with lemon juice. Combine the anchovies, mushrooms, bacon, bread crumbs, parsley, lemon rind, salt, pepper and egg yolk and mix well, adding a small amount of milk to moisten, if needed. Stuff veal with mushroom mixture and roll. Secure with string or skewers. Place in a roasting pan and add the butter and stock. Bake at 350 degrees for 1 hour and 40 minutes or until tender.

Mrs. Mitchell Callis, Orlando, Florida

ROAST STUFFED LOIN OF VEAL

3 1/2 lb. loin of veal	1 sm. onion, minced
2 c. bread crumbs	1/2 c. diced celery

2 tbsp. butter	1 tsp. salt
1/2 c. hot water	1/4 tsp. pepper
1/4 c. grated American cheese	4 bacon strips

Cut a pocket in the veal with a sharp knife. Combine the bread crumbs, onion and celery. Combine the butter and water and stir until melted. Stir into the onion mixture and add cheese, salt and pepper. Place the stuffing in pocket and sew closed or fasten with skewers. Place the veal on a rack in roasting pan and place the bacon on veal. Add enough water to partially cover the veal. Roast for 2 hours at 325 degrees. 8 servings.

Pearl Boulet, Crowley, Louisiana

VEAL POT ROAST

1 3-lb. boneless rolled shoulder of veal	1 tbsp. salt
1 1/2 tbsp. shortening	1/2 tsp. ground pepper
3/4 c. hot water	3 tbsp. flour
1 bay leaf	3 tbsp. cold water
3 tbsp. instant minced onion	1/4 to 1/2 tsp. dillseed
	1/2 c. sour cream

Brown the veal on all sides in shortening in a Dutch oven and place on a rack. Add hot water and bay leaf and cover. Cook over low heat for 2 hours. Sprinkle with onion, salt and pepper and cover. Cook for 30 minutes longer or until veal is tender. Remove veal to a platter. Mix the flour and cold water to a smooth paste and stir into liquid in Dutch oven. Blend in dillseed and cook until thickened. Stir in sour cream and heat through, but do not boil. Serve in gravy boat. Garnish veal with stuffed tomatoes. 6-8 servings.

Veal Pot Roast (above)

STUFFED LEG OF VEAL

1 4 to 5-lb. leg of veal, boned	Salt and pepper to taste
3 med. onions	2 egg yolks, beaten
1/2 lb. cooked calf liver	Butter
1 c. dry bread crumbs	1/2 pt. sour cream

Pound the veal out flat. Chop the onion and liver fine, add the bread crumbs, salt, pepper and egg yolks and mix well. Place on the veal and roll as for jelly roll. Tie with string and place in a roasting pan. Dot with butter. Bake at 350 degrees for 2 hours or until done. Place the sour cream in a saucepan and heat through. Pour over veal. 8 servings.

Mrs. Hamlin Tippins, Griffin, Georgia

VEAL PARMIGIANA

1/3 c. melted butter	2 8-oz. cans tomato sauce
3/4 tsp. salt	2 tsp. oregano
1/8 tsp. pepper	1/4 tsp. onion salt
1 c. finely crushed corn flakes	1/2 tsp. sugar
1/2 c. grated Parmesan cheese	6 3-in. square slices mozzarella
2 lb. veal cutlets or veal steaks	cheese
2 eggs, slightly beaten	

Pour the butter into a 13 1/2 x 8 3/4 x 1 3/4-inch baking dish. Combine the salt, pepper, corn flake crumbs and Parmesan cheese. Cut the veal cutlets into 6 pieces, dip into eggs, then dip into crumb mixture. Dip into eggs, dip into crumbs and place in butter in the baking dish. Bake at 400 degrees for 20 minutes. Turn veal and bake for about 20 minutes longer or until tender. Mix the tomato sauce, oregano, onion salt and sugar and heat to boiling point. Pour around veal and top each piece of veal with 1 slice mozzarella cheese. Return to oven and bake for about 3 minutes longer or until cheese melts. 6 servings.

Veal Parmigiana (above)

VEAL PALERMO

1/4 c. flour	Oil
1/2 c. grated Parmesan cheese	1 lge. onion, thinly sliced
1/2 tsp. salt	1 green pepper, thinly sliced
Dash of pepper	1/2 c. barbecue sauce
6 veal steaks	1 8-oz. can tomato sauce
1 egg, beaten	Dash of garlic salt

Combine the flour, cheese, salt and pepper. Dip the veal steaks in egg, then in seasoned flour. Brown in small amount of oil in a skillet. Place in a shallow baking dish and top with the onion and green pepper. Combine the barbecue sauce, tomato sauce and garlic salt and pour over the veal steaks. Sprinkle with additional cheese. Bake at 325 degrees for 35 minutes. 6 servings.

Pearl Scott, Gainesville, Florida

VEAL ITALIAN WITH ELBOW MACARONI

1/2 clove of garlic, minced	1 tsp. salt
1 sm. onion, chopped	3/4 tsp. dried oregano
2 tbsp. butter	1/4 tsp. pepper
2 lb. thin veal steak	1 8-oz. package elbow macaroni
2 c. tomato sauce	2 tbsp. snipped parsley
2 c. canned tomatoes	Grated Parmesan cheese

Saute the garlic and onion in butter in a skillet until lightly browned. Remove from skillet and set aside. Cut the veal in 8 pieces and saute in the same skillet until golden brown on both sides. Add the tomato sauce, tomatoes, salt, oregano, pepper and onion mixture and simmer for 30 minutes or until the veal is tender, stirring occasionally. Cook the macaroni according to package directions and drain. Place macaroni on a heated platter and top with the veal mixture. Sprinkle with the parsley and Parmesan cheese. 6 servings.

Linda Dawson, Pollocksville, North Carolina

PARSLIED VEAL STEAKS

1 1/2 lb. thin veal steak	1/8 tsp. pepper
2 tbsp. chopped onion	1 egg, beaten
2 tbsp. butter	2 c. soft bread crumbs
2 tsp. salt	2 tbsp. flour
2 tsp. sage (opt.)	1 tbsp. fat
2 tbsp. chopped parsley (opt.)	1 c. boiling water

Cut the veal steak into 6 portions. Cook the onion in butter in a saucepan until tender, then add salt, sage, parsley, pepper, egg and bread crumbs. Mix well and place 1/6 of the mixture on each steak. Fold the steaks over and fasten with small skewers. Roll in flour and brown in melted fat in a skillet. Add water and cover. Cook over low heat for 50 minutes, adding water as needed. May be baked at 400 degrees for about 1 hour. 6 servings.

Mrs. Thomas B. Turner, Emporia, Virginia

Stuffed Veal Birds in Sour Cream Gravy (below)

STUFFED VEAL BIRDS IN SOUR CREAM GRAVY

1/2 c. diced celery	1/4 c. milk
1/4 c. chopped onion	8 boneless veal cutlets
1/2 c. butter	1/3 c. flour
2 c. soft bread cubes	1/4 c. water
3/4 tsp. salt	1/4 c. white cooking wine
1/8 tsp. sage	1/2 pt. sour cream
Dash of pepper	1 4-oz. can mushrooms, drained
1 tbsp. chopped parsley	

Saute the celery and onion in 1/4 cup butter until onion is tender. Add the bread cubes, 1/4 teaspoon salt, sage, pepper, parsley and milk and toss lightly. Divide in 8 portions and place 1 portion in center of each cutlet. Roll veal around dressing and fasten with wooden picks or skewers. Dredge with flour and brown on all sides in remaining butter in a skillet. Add the water and wine and cover tightly. Cook over low heat for about 45 minutes or until veal is tender. Remove veal to a serving platter and keep warm. Blend remaining flour and sour cream and stir into liquid in skillet. Add mushrooms and remaining salt and cook, stirring constantly, until thickened. Serve with Veal Birds. 6-8 servings.

BREADED VEAL CHOPS

6 lge. veal chops	1 tsp. salt
2 c. cracker crumbs	1/2 c. oil
1 c. evaporated milk	

Roll the veal chops in the cracker crumbs, then dip in milk. Roll again in the cracker crumbs and sprinkle with salt. Refrigerate for 1 hour. Heat oil in a large, heavy skillet and add the chops. Fry until brown on both sides. 6 servings.

Ruby B. Edeburn, Bridgeport, West Virginia

VEAL CHOPS WITH RICE

6 veal chops	3 tbsp. chopped onion
Seasoned flour	3 tbsp. chopped green pepper
3 tbsp. fat	1 1/2 tsp. salt
3/4 c. rice	1/4 tsp. pepper
3 c. tomato juice	1/2 tsp. marjoram

Trim the bone from the veal chops and dredge the chops with seasoned flour. Melt the fat in a frypan and brown the chops on both sides. Add the remaining ingredients and cover. Simmer for 45 minutes without removing cover.

Mrs. Floyd O'Neal, Smiley, Texas

VEAL CHOP BROIL

1/2 c. catsup	1 clove of garlic, minced
1/3 c. vinegar	1 tbsp. prepared mustard
1/4 c. brown sugar	1 tbsp. oil
2 tbsp. soy sauce	4 veal chops, 3/4 in. thick

Combine the catsup, vinegar, brown sugar, soy sauce, garlic, mustard and oil. Place the veal chops in a shallow baking pan and pour the catsup mixture over chops. Refrigerate for 2 hours, turning chops occasionally. Place the chops on a broiler pan and place the broiler pan 3 to 6 inches from heat. Broil the chops for about 10 minutes on each side. 4 servings.

Elfreda G. Conard, Dover, Delaware

VEAL CUBES WITH CORNMEAL DUMPLINGS

1 1/2 lb. veal stew meat	1 c. diced potatoes
Flour	1/2 c. sliced celery
4 c. tomato juice	1/2 c. chopped onion
2 tsp. salt	1 10-oz. package corn bread mix
1 1/2 tsp. monosodium glutamate	2 tbsp. minced parsley
4 dashes of hot sauce	Milk

Cut the veal into 1-inch cubes and dredge with flour. Brown over low heat in small amount of fat in a heavy skillet. Add the tomato juice, salt, monosodium glutamate and hot sauce and cover. Simmer for 1 hour. Add the vegetables and cover. Cook for about 30 minutes or until vegetables are tender. Prepare corn bread mix according to package directions, adding parsley and using only 1/3 cup milk. Drop by rounded spoonfuls into veal mixture and cover. Simmer for 10 to 12 minutes or until dumplings are done.

Mrs. A. E. Atkinson, Sr., Darlington, South Carolina

VEAL STROGANOFF

4 1/2 lb. veal	1 c. boiling water
6 tbsp. flour	1 tsp. dry mustard
3 med. onions, thinly sliced	3 tsp. paprika
1 clove of garlic, minced	3 tbsp. chopped parsley
1/2 c. butter	1 sm. can mushrooms, chopped
2 beef bouillon cubes	1 c. sour cream

Cut the veal into thin strips and dredge with flour. Brown the onions and garlic in 1/4 cup butter. Place the onions and garlic in a bowl with bouillon cubes, add the boiling water and stir until the bouillon cubes are dissolved. Add the mustard, paprika, parsley and mushrooms. Place the remaining butter in the skillet and brown the veal. Add the bouillon mixture and cover. Simmer for 1 hour and 30 minutes. Add the sour cream and simmer for 5 minutes longer. 8 servings.

Mrs. Goebel Bennett, Mayfield, Kentucky

GLAZED VEAL

2 lb. boneless veal	1/2 c. lemon juice
1/2 c. unsulphured molasses	1/2 tsp. salt
1/4 c. soy sauce	2 tsp. monosodium glutamate
2 scallions, chopped	1/2 tsp. ginger
2 cloves of garlic, crushed	1 1/2 c. water

Cut the veal into 1-inch cubes. Combine remaining ingredients in a deep bowl. Add the veal and refrigerate for several hours or overnight. Turn the veal with marinade into a large skillet and place over medium heat. Bring to a boil and reduce heat. Simmer for 30 minutes or until veal is tender. Uncover and cook over high heat for 20 to 25 minutes or until liquid is reduced and veal is glazed. Serve with rice. 6-8 servings.

Glazed Veal (above)

126

SPAGHETTI WITH VEAL AND PEPPERS

2 lb. boneless veal shoulder	2 8-oz. cans tomato sauce
Flour	Salt
1/4 c. butter or margarine	1 1/2 tsp. basil leaves
1/3 c. olive oil	1/4 to 1/2 tsp. oregano
4 med. green peppers	1/8 tsp. freshly ground pepper
2 sm. onions, sliced	4 to 6 qt. boiling water
4 cloves of garlic, minced	1 lb. spaghetti
2 1-lb. 3-oz. cans tomatoes	

Cut the veal in strips and dredge with flour. Brown in the butter and oil in a large skillet and remove from skillet. Cut the green pepper in strips. Saute the green peppers and onions in same skillet for about 5 minutes. Add the veal, garlic, tomatoes, tomato sauce, 1 1/2 teaspoons salt, herbs and pepper and cover skillet. Simmer for 1 hour, stirring occasionally. Add 2 tablespoons salt to boiling water and add spaghetti gradually so that water continues to boil. Cook, stirring occasionally, until tender, then drain in a colander. Serve with veal mixture. 8 servings.

Photograph for this recipe on page 116.

CUTLET ITALIANO

1 10-oz. package frozen breaded veal cutlets	1 4-oz. can sliced mushrooms
	Grated Parmesan cheese to taste (opt.)
2 tbsp. butter or margarine	1 c. cocktail vegetable juice

Brown the veal cutlets in the butter in a skillet according to package directions and remove from skillet. Drain the mushrooms, add to the drippings in skillet and cook until brown. Place the veal cutlets in skillet with mushrooms and sprinkle with Parmesan cheese. Pour vegetable juice over all. Cook over low heat until the cutlets are tender and the sauce is thick. 4 servings.

Mrs. Jonnie P. Bradshaw, Ozark, Alabama

VEAL CUTLETS IN CASSEROLE

3 veal cutlets	1/4 c. cooking sherry
1/2 lb. mushrooms	2 tbsp. parsley flakes
1 can cream of mushroom soup	2 tbsp. minced onion

Saute the veal cutlets in a skillet until golden brown. Remove from the skillet and place in a casserole. Saute the mushrooms in the same skillet and place over veal. Combine remaining ingredients and blend well. Pour over the mushrooms and cover casserole. Bake for 1 hour at 350 degrees. 3 servings.

Mrs. Margaret Hamilton, Wetumpka, Alabama

CHINESE VEAL

1 1/2 lb. ground veal	1/2 c. rice
1/4 c. chopped onion	1/4 c. soy sauce
3 tbsp. bacon fat	1 can chicken noodle soup
1 c. peas	1 can cream of mushroom soup
1 c. finely chopped celery	3 c. water

Brown the veal and onion in bacon fat in a skillet. Add the remaining ingredients and pour into a large baking dish. Bake at 350 degrees for 1 hour, stirring every 15 minutes. 10 servings.

Mrs. William Nelson, Carthage, Mississippi

MINIATURE MEATBALLS

2 med. onions, sliced	1 tbsp. chopped parsley
2 tbsp. salad oil	1 tsp. oregano
1 No. 2 1/2 can tomatoes	1/4 tsp. cloves
1 6-oz. can tomato paste	4 bay leaves
1 1/2 c. water	

Brown the onions in oil in a large skillet, then add the remaining ingredients. Simmer for 1 hour and 30 minutes.

Meatballs

1 lge. onion, chopped	2 tbsp. grated Parmesan cheese
2 tbsp. salad oil	1 c. bread crumbs
1 1/2 lb. ground veal	2 eggs
1/2 tsp. garlic salt	Salt and pepper to taste

Brown the onion in oil in a skillet, remove onion from skillet and set aside. Combine the remaining ingredients in a large bowl and add the onion. Shape into 1-inch balls and brown in remaining oil in the skillet. Place meatballs in the tomato sauce and simmer for about 1 hour. Meatballs may be removed from sauce and served with cocktail picks or meatballs and sauce may be served over cooked spaghetti or noodles. 6 servings.

Leoda Mestrovic, Wellsburg, West Virginia

BAKED VEAL CUTLETS

1 pkg. onion soup mix	2 lb. veal cutlets
2 1/2 c. boiling water	Flour

Stir the soup mix into boiling water. Dredge the veal with flour and pound well. Cut the veal into individual portions and saute in small amount of fat in a skillet until lightly browned. Place in a baking dish and add the soup mixture. Bake at 350 degrees for 30 minutes.

Mrs. Roberta Craig, Houston, Texas

VEAL ROLLS

1/2 c. crushed bleu cheese crackers	1 sm. onion, grated
1/2 c. milk	1 tsp. salt
1 lb. ground veal	Pepper to taste
	8 slices bacon

Soak the cracker crumbs in milk until softened. Add the veal, onion, salt and pepper and blend thoroughly. Divide into 8 equal portions and shape each portion into a rectangle. Wrap each rectangle with a slice of bacon and secure at ends with toothpicks. Place on rack in a broiler pan and place broiler pan 4 inches from heat. Broil until bacon is crisp. Turn and broil until bacon is crisp. 8 servings.

Anna Mae Vaughn, Berry, Kentucky

BAKED EGGPLANT WITH VEAL

1/2 c. flour	1 lb. ground veal
1 3/4 tsp. salt	1/4 lb. mushrooms, chopped
1/4 tsp. pepper	1 tbsp. finely chopped onion
1 egg, slightly beaten	1/2 c. soft bread crumbs
1 tbsp. milk	3 tbsp. grated Parmesan cheese
1 med. eggplant, peeled	2 med. tomatoes
1/3 c. salad oil	

Mix the flour, 3/4 teaspoon salt and 1/8 teaspoon pepper. Combine egg and milk and mix well. Cut the eggplant in 6 crosswise slices and dip into flour mixture. Dip into egg mixture, then dip into flour mixture again. Reserve remaining egg mixture. Heat 3 tablespoons oil in a large skillet and brown eggplant on both sides. Place in a 9 x 13-inch baking pan. Cook the veal, mushrooms and onion in remaining oil until brown. Remove from heat and mix in bread crumbs, cheese, remaining salt and pepper and reserved egg mixture. Spoon over eggplant slices and cover baking pan with foil. Bake in 350-degree oven for 20 minutes and uncover. Cut each tomato into 3 slices and place over veal mixture. Bake for 15 minutes longer and garnish with parsley, if desired. 6 servings.

Baked Eggplant with Veal (above)

LOAF DE VEAU

2 eggs, beaten	5 drops of hot sauce
1/2 c. milk	1 1/2 lb. ground veal
1 1/2 tsp. salt	1/4 c. chopped onion
1/2 tsp. pepper	1 c. crushed potato chips
1 tsp. Worcestershire sauce	

Combine the eggs, milk, salt, pepper, Worcestershire sauce and hot sauce in a large bowl. Add the veal and onion and mix well. Add the crushed chips and mix lightly. Press into loaf pan. Bake at 350 degrees for 45 minutes. 6 servings.

Polly Lee Ramsey, McColl, South Carolina

VEAL SOUP

1 lb. ground veal	1 1/2 c. sliced carrots
Salt and pepper to taste	1 1/2 c. sliced celery
1 1/2 tsp. Italian seasoning	1/3 c. chopped parsley
8 c. water	Grated Romano cheese
1 lge. onion, chopped	

Season the ground veal with salt and pepper and 1/2 teaspoon Italian seasoning and mix well. Shape into marble-sized balls. Place in a heavy saucepan, add the water and bring to a boil. Add the vegetables, remaining Italian seasoning, salt and pepper and cover. Cook over low heat for about 2 hours. Ladle into soup bowls and sprinkle with cheese.

Mrs. W. A. Ferrari, San Antonio, Texas

VEAL-LIMA RAGOUT

1 lb. ground veal	1 c. sliced carrots
2 tbsp. fat	2 c. diced celery
2 1/2 c. canned tomatoes	1 bay leaf
1 No. 303 can lima beans	1/2 tsp. garlic salt
4 c. hot water	1/2 tsp. pepper
2 tsp. salt	1/4 c. chopped parsley

Brown the ground veal in fat in a Dutch oven. Add the remaining ingredients except parsley, bring to a boil and cover. Simmer for 30 minutes. Remove cover and simmer for 15 minutes longer. Garnish with parsley. 6 servings.

Mrs. Helen Butler, Cameron, Texas

RAGOUT DE VEAU

1 1/2 lb. boned veal shoulder	1/8 tsp. thyme
3 c. water	1 bay leaf
1 1/2 tsp. monosodium glutamate	1 sprig of parsley
3/4 tsp. salt	8 sm. onions

6 carrots, halved
1/4 c. butter or margarine
1/2 lb. small mushrooms
2 tbsp. flour

2 egg yolks
2 tbsp. lemon juice
1 tbsp. snipped dill

Cut the veal shoulder into 1 1/2-inch cubes and place in a kettle. Add the water, monosodium glutamate, salt, thyme, bay leaf and parsley and bring to a boil. Cover and simmer for 30 minutes. Add the onions and carrots and simmer for 30 minutes longer or until the veal is tender. Drain and reserve stock. Heat 2 tablespoons butter in a skillet. Add the mushrooms and cook over low heat for 5 minutes. Reserve mushrooms. Add enough water to reserved stock to make 2 cups liquid. Melt remaining butter in a saucepan and blend in flour. Stir in stock and cook, stirring constantly, until mixture comes to a boil and thickens. Beat egg yolks and lemon juice together. Stir in small amount of the stock mixture, then stir back into the saucepan. Cook over low heat, stirring constantly, until thickened. Do not boil. Add to veal mixture and heat through over low heat. Sprinkle with dill and garnish with reserved mushrooms. 4 servings.

Mrs. Charles Bell, Hereford, Texas

VEAL-MUSHROOM STEW

1 1/2 lb. veal, cut in cubes
Oil
1/2 tsp. basil
1 clove of garlic, minced
1 tsp. onion powder
1/4 tsp. thyme
1 lge. can mushrooms and
    liquid

1 can beef consomme
1 8-oz. can tomato sauce
Diced carrots to taste
Diced potatoes to taste
Diced onions to taste

Brown the veal in small amount of oil. Add basil, garlic, onion powder, thyme, mushrooms, beef consomme and tomato sauce and bring to a boil. Simmer for 2 hours. Add the carrots, potatoes and onions and simmer for 30 minutes longer. Thicken with a small amount of flour mixed with water, if desired.

Mrs. Elizabeth P. Tullos, Hattiesburg, Mississippi

VEAL-VEGETABLE SALAD

2 c. diced cooked veal
1 sm. onion, minced
1/4 c. minced celery
1/2 c. stuffed olives

1 tsp. lemon juice
1 tbsp. mayonnaise
1 head lettuce

Place the veal in a bowl. Add the onion and celery and mix well. Cut the olives in halves and add to the veal mixture. Mix the lemon juice with the mayonnaise and fold into the veal mixture. Line a salad bowl with lettuce leaves. Place the veal mixture in lettuce. 4 servings.

Mrs. W. D. Smith, Selma, Alabama

Graustark Venison (page 136)

game meat

T hey left at dawn.

John, Bobby, Mike — the men in your family — filled with hopes for conquest, packed their hunting gear and left home while the sun was still low on the horizon.

Now, they have returned; it is time for you to take over. From their day of hunting, your men have brought you their kill. They now expect you to turn what they have brought home into a hunter's feast.

The sport of game hunting is a typical pastime in the South. Southerners traditionally have proven themselves among the best hunters in the country.

But sometimes, the lady of the house finds it difficult to match the feats of the hunter fresh from the field.

Now you can take as much pride in preparing a feast of game meat as the men do in bringing that game home.

The recipes in this section are for game meat entrees that Southern women take pride in serving. They come to you from Southern homes in which game hunting is a favorite sport. From venison to squirrel, the selections run a wide gamut of delicious game meat recipes. Some are unusual, but all will delight the members of your family, especially the sportsmen.

In the pioneer days of the United States, game was the primary source of meat for the family dining table. A good cook knew hundreds of ways to prepare rabbit, squirrel, opossum, raccoon, and the most prized delicacy of all, venison. The few domesticated animals were far too precious to be killed for their meat.

Now all that has changed. Growing cattle, hogs, and other animals for their meat has become big business. The consequent loss of game from dining tables has been unfortunate. Game is high in needed protein — far higher than domestic animals — and is a taste-treat welcomed by families and guests alike.

Many cooks are afraid to prepare game because they have heard tales about its dryness, toughness, or unpleasant flavor. It is true that the meat from

general directions
FOR GAME MEAT

game is far less tender than that from domestic animals, especially immediately after the game has been killed. But properly stored — "hung" is the usual term — the flesh becomes tender and acquires the delicious flavor which makes it delightful eating.

Cooking game is easy once a few basic tricks have been mastered. Game animals have far less fat than their domestic counterparts and must be well-larded before cooking. Failure to lard produces the dry, tough, sinewy meat which gives game such a bad reputation. The larding material should be matched to the game — delicately-flavored fats for the delicately-flavored small animals and the heavier fats for the larger game. Investment in a 12-inch to 15-inch larding needle will pay dividends in flavor and eating pleasure.

Another basic trick in cooking game is to use herbs and spices — but sparingly! Marjoram, rosemary, thyme, basil, and oregano go well with everything. If fresh herbs are hard to find, try using 1/4 teaspoon of dried herbs as equivalent to a teaspoon of fresh. Some game may have too strong a flavor of sage. This can be overcome by using thyme. And parsley is not only decorative but is full of many needed minerals.

Bear meat should be marinated in oil and vinegar or in wine for at least two days before cooking. All bear meat, except black bear, is edible and prized for its delicious flavor. Before cooking, all the fat should be removed from the meat. If left on, it becomes an unappetizing, slightly rancid mass. Bear may be roasted or broiled, just like fine beef. It should be thoroughly cooked before eating as it may contain some intestinal parasites harmful to man. Just cook it as you would pork, and it will be delightful and safe fare.

Venison — the meat of elk, deer, moose, or caribou — is similar to beef and veal. However it is of finer texture and has far less fat marbling. As with bear, all fat should be removed before cooking. Left on, it becomes unappealing and tallow-like. Venison should be very well-larded, then roasted. Salting before cooking toughens the meat, but sugaring tenderizes it. Venison should be seared in a 500-degree oven, then roasted at about 300 to 350 degrees, basting frequently, for a minimum of 20 minutes per pound.

More common than either bear or venison are the small game animals — rabbits, hares, squirrels, chipmunks, beaver, raccoon, and opossum. Young small game animals may be either fried or baked. In fact, rabbit and squirrel may be substituted for chicken in almost any recipe. Older animals must be parboiled before baking. If marinated in olive oil and wine vinegar before parboiling, they will become tender. Before baking small game, rub the inside with lemon and melted butter; cook in a slow oven, basting with any one of the usual basting mixtures. Lemon juice and current jelly is a particularly good basting combination for small game. If fried, small game should be thoroughly dusted with a flour-and-cinnamon mixture before cooking.

Squirrels at one time were so popular that the famous Kentucky squirrel gun was developed especially for squirrel hunting. Gray squirrels are preferred eating. Red ones are considered too small and too gamey in flavor. If they are to be baked, squirrels should be thoroughly larded with bacon and roasted for one to one and a half hours in a moderate oven. Squirrels may also be dredged in flour and fried until browned, partially covered with water and simmered for about one hour. One of the favorite ways to serve squirrel is in Brunswick stew, a savory blend of squirrel, potatoes, onions, lima beans, and tomatoes.

Rabbit is another favorite small game animal. Its milk-flavored and finely-grained meat can be cooked like chicken. It is most often fried. But it may also be marinated and cooked in the marinade, as in the famous German dish, Hasenpfeffer. Older rabbits are best served in stews or pies — "smothered" is the usual term. Rabbit must be well-larded before cooking as — like squirrel — it has little natural fat.

Opossum, a favorite Southern game animal, is highly prized for his light-colored, fine-grained meat. Because the meat is tender, opossum may be roasted, stewed, or broiled. Most of the fat should be removed before cooking. An unusual way to prepare opossum is to bake it in a blanket of moist clay over a bed of coals. This is especially good on camping trips.

Raccoon is similar to opossum, but its meat is coarser. It should be cooked by braising for 3 to 4 hours.

GRAUSTARK VENISON

1 6 to 7-lb. leg of venison	6 or 7 strips salt pork
Salt to taste	3/4 c. melted butter
2 c. dry red wine	2 tbsp. flour
2 med. onions, quartered	1 c. beef broth
2 med. carrots, sliced	3 lb. small potatoes
4 sprigs of parsley	White pepper to taste
2 bay leaves	Snipped parsley to taste
10 peppercorns	2 10-oz. packages frozen
4 whole cloves	Brussels sprouts, thawed
Dash of thyme	1/4 c. chopped walnuts

Season the venison with salt and place in a shallow pan. Combine the wine, onions, carrots, parsley, bay leaves, peppercorns, cloves and thyme and pour over the venison. Refrigerate for 24 hours, turning occasionally. Remove venison from marinade and strain and reserve marinade. Place venison on rack in a shallow baking pan and place salt pork across venison. Roast in 450-degree oven for 25 minutes. Reduce temperature to 325 degrees and roast for about 2 hours longer or until venison is medium rare, basting frequently with half the reserved marinade. Remove venison to a hot platter. Combine remaining marinade with pan drippings in a saucepan and bring to a boil. Blend 2 tablespoons butter with flour and stir into marinade. Stir in broth slowly and cook, stirring constantly, until mixture comes to a boil. Cook for 1 minute longer. Peel potatoes and cut in half. Cook in boiling, salted water for 15 to 20 minutes or until tender. Drain and toss with 6 tablespoons butter, white pepper, salt and parsley. Saute the Brussels sprouts in remaining butter for 10 minutes. Add the walnuts and cook for 5 minutes. Arrange potatoes and Brussels sprouts around venison and serve with the gravy. 6-8 servings.

Photograph for this recipe on page 132

VENISON POT ROAST

1 3 to 5-lb. venison roast	3 tbsp. fat
1/2 tsp. pepper	4 to 6 sm. onions
2 tsp. salt	1 c. water
1/2 c. flour	

Soak the venison roast in cold, salted water for several hours or overnight. Drain and season with pepper and salt. Dredge with flour and brown on all sides in hot fat in a Dutch oven. Add the onions and water and cover. Simmer until tender. Potatoes and carrots may be added about 20 minutes before the roast is done.

Mrs. Fred Moon, Pinehurst, Georgia

ROAST VENISON

1 5-lb. leg of venison	Strips of bacon or salt pork
Salt and pepper to taste	1 c. red wine
Garlic cloves, cut in half (opt.)	

Wipe the venison with a damp cloth and sprinkle with salt and pepper. Cut slits at 2-inch intervals over venison and insert garlic in the slits. Cover venison with bacon. Place venison in a baking pan and pour the wine over venison. Bake at 325 degrees for 15 to 20 minutes per pound for rare, 20 to 25 minutes for medium-rare or 30 minutes for well done, basting frequently with pan drippings.

Mrs. H. H. Tippins, Griffin, Georgia

VENISON ROAST WITH SAUCE

1 can tomato sauce	2 tbsp. sugar
Salt and pepper to taste	Worcestershire sauce to taste
1 sm. onion, chopped fine	1 vension roast
2 tbsp. vinegar	Sliced bacon

Combine the tomato sauce, salt, pepper, onion, vinegar, sugar and Worcestershire sauce. Place the venison roast on a large sheet of foil in a baking pan and cover the roast with bacon. Pour the tomato sauce mixture over roast and fold and seal the foil. Bake at 300 degrees for 3 hours.

Mrs. Edgar H. McCall, Horse Shoe, North Carolina

ELK ROAST

1 elk roast	Celery salt
8 sm. whole potatoes	Onion salt
8 sm. whole carrots	1/2 c. grape wine vinegar
8 sm. whole onions	

Place the elk roast in a baking pan and surround with vegetables. Sprinkle with seasonings. Bake at 325 degrees for 3 hours basting frequently with vinegar. Venison may be substituted for elk.

Venison Roast with Sauce (above)

137

ANTELOPE STEAKS SUPREME

3 antelope round steaks, 3/4 in. thick	Dash of pepper
2 tsp. salt	Dash of garlic salt
1/4 c. vinegar	Flour
1 bay leaf (opt.)	2 to 3 tbsp. cooking oil
1 clove of garlic, minced	1 can cream of chicken soup

Place the antelope steaks in a shallow pan and cover with water. Add the salt, vinegar, bay leaf and garlic and soak for 3 hours or overnight. Drain steaks and sprinkle with the pepper and garlic salt. Dredge with flour. Brown on both sides in oil in lightly greased skillet and cover. Cook over low heat for 45 minutes or until tender, turning occasionally. Add the soup and 1 soup can water and cover. Simmer for 15 to 20 minutes. Gravy may be served over rice or potatoes. Mushroom soup may be substituted for chicken soup. 6 servings.

Mrs. Kenneth Underwood, Montgomery, Alabama

VENISON STEAK

Venison steak	Thyme to taste
1 onion, chopped	1 bay leaf
1 carrot, chopped	2 or 3 whole cloves
1 stalk celery, chopped	1 c. vinegar
1 leaf parsley	Flour

Remove all fat from the venison steak and pound well. Place in a shallow baking dish. Cook the onion, carrot and celery in a skillet in small amount of fat until tender. Place parsley, thyme, bay leaf and cloves in a cheesecloth bag and place in the skillet. Add the vinegar and simmer for 20 minutes. Pour over the venison and refrigerate for 12 to 24 hours. Drain the venison and rinse in cold water. Drain again and dredge with flour. Fry in small amount of hot fat until brown and add 1 cup water. Bake at 350 degrees until tender.

Ruth Barnes, Beaver Dam, Kentucky

BARBECUED VENISON RIB STEAKS

6 venison rib steaks	1 tsp. salt
Pepper to taste	1 tsp. chili powder
1/2 c. onion slices	1/3 c. Worcestershire sauce
1 thinly sliced lemon	Dash of hot sauce
1 c. catsup	1/4 c. vinegar
1 c. water	

Place the venison steaks in a Dutch oven and season with pepper. Cover with the onion and place the lemon slices over onion. Bake at 400 degrees for about 15 minutes. Mix the remaining ingredients in a saucepan and bring to a boil. Pour over the venison. Reduce temperature to 350 degrees and bake for 1 hour or until tender, basting with sauce several times and adding water if sauce becomes dry. 6 servings.

Mrs. Zelda Worley, Wesley, Arkansas

STRATTON-STYLE DEER STEAKS

2 lb. deer loin, cut 1/2 in. thick
1 c. milk
4 tbsp. seasoned flour

2 tbsp. shortening
1 c. water

Soak the deer loin in milk for several hours. Drain and dredge with the seasoned flour. Brown in shortening in 10-inch skillet. Add water and bring to a boil. Reduce heat and cover. Simmer for 2 hours or until tender.

Mrs. Howard Stratton, Cookson, Oklahoma

TENDERLOIN DEER STEAK

1 deer tenderloin
Milk
Salt

Flour
Shortening

Slice the deer tenderloin crosswise into steaks and pound well. Place in a bowl and cover with milk. Sprinkle with 1 teaspoon salt and let stand for 30 minutes. Drain and sprinkle with salt to taste. Dredge with flour. Fry in small amount of shortening until lightly browned and serve hot.

Mrs. Mary Mathis, Lometa, Texas

BARBECUED DEER STEAKS

2 lb. deer steaks
1 tsp. salt
1/2 tsp. pepper
Flour

3 tbsp. butter
1 lge. onion, minced
1 bottle barbecue sauce
1/2 c. white wine

Cut the deer steaks in serving pieces and season with the salt and pepper. Dredge with flour and brown in the butter in a skillet. Layer the steaks, onion and barbecue sauce in a casserole until all ingredients are used. Pour the wine over top and cover casserole. Bake at 350 degrees for 1 hour. 6 servings.

Mrs. Edgar Moser, Memphis, Tennessee

VENISON CHOPS

6 venison chops, well trimmed
Salt and pepper to taste
1/4 tsp. onion salt

1/2 c. flour
3 tbsp. shortening

Season the venison chops with salt, pepper and onion salt and dredge with flour. Cover and cook over low heat in shortening in a skillet for 1 hour, turning occasionally and adding a small amount of water if necessary. Remove cover and brown the chops on both sides. 6 servings.

Mrs. Bill Scott, Griffin, Georgia

VANCOUVER ISLAND VENISON

3 tbsp. margarine	1 tsp. salt
1 tsp. mustard	1/4 tsp. pepper
1 tsp. brown sugar	4 tomatoes, sliced
2 onions, chopped	1 c. sliced mushrooms
2 lb. venison	1 tsp. vinegar
1/4 c. flour	

Melt the margarine in a large saucepan. Add the mustard, sugar and onions and cook until the onions are tender. Cut the venison into small pieces. Mix the flour with salt and pepper and dredge the venison with the flour mixture. Add to onion mixture and add the tomatoes and mushrooms. Sprinkle with the vinegar. Simmer for 3 hours, stirring occasionally.

Mrs. Freylon Hughes, Searcy, Arkansas

WILD GAME STROGANOFF

1 1/2 lb. elk	1 med. onion, chopped
3 tbsp. flour	1 can mushroom soup
2 tsp. salt	1/2 soup can water
1/2 tsp. pepper	1 can button mushrooms
1 tsp. paprika	1 c. sour cream
Dash of garlic salt (opt.)	

Cut the elk into small cubes. Combine the flour, salt, pepper, paprika and garlic salt in a paper bag, add the elk and shake well. Brown the elk and onion in small amount of bacon drippings in a skillet. Mix the soup with water and add to the skillet. Simmer until the elk is tender. Add the mushrooms and sour cream and heat through. Serve over hot rice. 4 servings.

Mrs. S. W. Johnson, Montgomery, Alabama

OZARK-STYLE VENISON STROGANOFF

1 1/2 lb. venison	1 can tomato soup
Flour	6 drops of hot sauce
2 tbsp. shortening	1 tbsp. Worcestershire sauce
1 6-oz. can mushrooms	1/2 tsp. salt
1/2 onion, minced	1 1/2 c. sour cream
1 clove of garlic, minced	

Cut the venison into 1 1/2-inch cubes and dredge with flour. Brown in hot shortening in a skillet. Drain the mushrooms and reserve liquid. Add the onion, garlic and mushrooms to the venison. Combine the soup, reserved mushroom liquid and seasonings and pour over the venison mixture. Simmer for 1 hour, stirring occasionally. Stir in sour cream just before serving and heat through, but do not boil. Serve over rice or mashed potatoes. 6 servings.

Mrs. Virgil Chester, Pocahontas, Arkansas

DEERBURGER MEAT LOAF

2 lb. ground deer	3 eggs
2 lb. bulk pork sausage	1 c. barbecue sauce
2 med. onions, finely chopped	1 tsp. salt
1 1/2 c. cracker crumbs	1/2 tsp. pepper
1/2 c. evaporated milk	1 8-oz. can tomato sauce

Combine the deer, sausage, onions and crumbs and mix well. Add the milk, eggs, barbecue sauce, salt, pepper and 1/2 can tomato sauce and blend well. Let stand for 15 minutes. Shape into a loaf and place in a greased baking pan. Bake at 350 degrees for 30 minutes. Top with remaining tomato sauce and bake for 1 hour longer or until done. 8 servings.

Mrs. Roy Griffin, Blackwell, Arkansas

VENISON CASSEROLE

1 lb. ground venison	1 tbsp. chili powder
1 green pepper, chopped	1 can tomato soup
1 onion, chopped	1 can mushroom soup
1 pkg. noodles	1 can cream-style corn
Salt and pepper to taste	1 1/2 c. grated cheese

Combine the venison, green pepper and onion in a skillet and cook until brown. Cook the noodles according to package directions and drain. Add to the venison mixture. Add the salt, pepper, chili powder, tomato soup, mushroom soup, cream-style corn and 1 cup grated cheese and mix well. Pour into a greased 2-quart casserole and sprinkle with remaining grated cheese. Bake at 275 degrees until heated through. Ground beef may be substituted for venison. 12 servings.

Mrs. D. H. Spearman, Easley, South Carolina

CHILI DEER

1 lb. ground pork	2 tbsp. vinegar
5 lb. ground deer	1 c. catsup
3 lge. onions, chopped	1 c. tomato sauce
4 cloves of garlic, crushed	2 1/2 tbsp. chili powder
2 sm. chili peppers, minced	4 No. 303 cans chili beans
1/2 box cumin seed	Salt to taste
6 c. water	

Combine the pork and deer in a large skillet and cook until brown, stirring frequently. Add the remaining ingredients and mix well. Simmer for 30 minutes or until most of the liquid has evaporated. 12 servings.

Mrs. Richard Madison, Montgomery, Alabama

VENISON SOUP

1 lb. venison, cut in cubes	3 bay leaves
1 c. diced turnips	1/2 tsp. thyme
1/2 c. minced parsley	1 can tomato paste
1 c. minced onion	3 tsp. sugar
2 c. diced celery	Salt and pepper to taste
3 qt. beef stock	

Combine all ingredients in a large kettle. Cook over low heat for 2 hours.

Mrs. Gilbert Davis, Montgomery, Alabama

RABBIT STEW

1 3 1/2-lb. rabbit	1/4 tsp. thyme
1 c. red wine vinegar	3/4 tsp. hot sauce
1 c. red table wine	1 c. flour
1 c. sliced onions	1/2 c. shortening
3 bay leaves	1 c. water or stock
3 tsp. salt	2 tsp. sugar
1/2 tsp. cloves	

Cut the rabbit into serving pieces. Combine the vinegar, wine, onions, bay leaves, 2 teaspoons salt, cloves, thyme and hot sauce and mix well. Add rabbit and refrigerate for 2 days. Drain the rabbit and strain and reserve marinade. Combine the flour and remaining salt and coat rabbit pieces. Heat the shortening in a large skillet and brown rabbit on all sides. Drain off fat. Add reserved marinade and water and cover. Simmer for about 45 minutes or until tender, stirring occasionally, then add sugar. 3-4 servings.

Rabbit Stew (above)

MEXICAN RABBIT

1 rabbit, disjointed	2 c. corn
1 tsp. parsley	1 No. 303 can tomatoes
1 tsp. rosemary	1 c. minced black olives
1 tsp. thyme	2 tsp. chili powder
1 bay leaf	Salt and pepper to taste
2 peppercorns	2 c. yellow cornmeal
1 garlic clove, minced	1 egg yolk
1/2 c. minced shallots	

Place the rabbit, parsley, rosemary, thyme, bay leaf and peppercorns in a large saucepan and add enough water to cover. Bring to a boil and simmer for 30 minutes or until the rabbit is tender. Drain rabbit and reserve 1 cup liquid. Remove rabbit from bones. Saute the garlic and shallots in small amount of fat in a skillet until tender, then add the rabbit, corn, tomatoes, olives, chili powder, salt and pepper. Simmer for 20 minutes. Combine the cornmeal and egg yolk. Strain the reserved liquid, add to cornmeal mixture and mix well. Stir into the rabbit mixture and spoon into a greased casserole. Bake at 325 degrees for 40 minutes or until set. 6 servings.

Mrs. Wallace Browder, Houston, Texas

HARVEST RABBIT WITH PUMPKIN

3 rabbits, disjointed	1/2 tsp. allspice
Salt and pepper to taste	2 c. diced pumpkin or cushaw
2 tbsp. lemon juice	2 pkg. frozen mixed vegetables

Cook the rabbits in a small amount of fat in a deep heavy skillet until brown. Add enough water to cover, salt, pepper, lemon juice and allspice and bring to a boil. Simmer for 1 hour or until rabbits are tender. Remove rabbits from bones and place back in skillet. Add the pumpkin and mixed vegetables and simmer for 30 minutes longer or until vegetables are done. 6 servings.

Mr. Henry Hamilton, Wetumpka, Alabama

HUNTER'S-STYLE RABBIT

1 rabbit, disjointed	1 tsp. curry powder
1 c. olive or salad oil	1 tsp. thyme
1 clove of garlic, halved	2 tsp. salt
1 c. flour	1/2 tsp. pepper
2 tbsp. dry mustard	1 c. light cream

Rub the rabbit with olive oil, place in a bowl and refrigerate overnight. Rub rabbit with garlic. Combine the flour, mustard, curry powder, thyme, salt and pepper in a paper bag and shake the rabbit in bag until coated. Fry in oil in a skillet until golden brown. Add the cream and cover skillet. Simmer for 1 hour or until tender. Place rabbit on a hot platter and pour cream sauce over the rabbit. 5 servings.

Mrs. Charles Glascow, Griffin, Georgia

MUSTARD-BEAR STEAKS

1 c. tarragon vinegar	Salt and pepper to taste
2 bay leaves	4 tbsp. dry mustard
1 c. red wine	Flour
1 c. water	2 c. beef stock
6 sm. bear steaks, 1 in. thick	

Combine the first 4 ingredients. Place the bear steaks in a bowl and pour the wine mixture over steaks. Marinate in refrigerator for 24 hours, turning steaks occasionally. Drain the steaks and reserve 1/2 cup marinade. Wipe the steaks dry and pound the salt, pepper and mustard into steaks. Dredge with flour and brown on both sides in small amount of hot fat in a Dutch oven. Add the beef stock and reserved marinade and cover. Simmer for 1 hour or until steaks are tender, adding water as needed. 6 servings.

Mrs. Dennis Smith, Grand Prairie, Texas

SAVORY BEAR

1 pt. tarragon vinegar	2 lb. bear meat, cut in cubes
2 peppercorns	1 c. minced shallots
3 bay leaves	Salt and pepper to taste
1 stick cinnamon	Flour
2 onions, quartered	1 pt. water
1/2 tsp. thyme	1 stick butter
1/2 tsp. basil	2 tbsp. Worcestershire sauce
1/2 tsp. rosemary	1 lge. can sliced mushrooms
1 c. minced celery	

Combine the vinegar, peppercorns, bay leaves, cinnamon, onions, thyme, basil, rosemary and celery and pour over the bear meat in a bowl. Marinate in refrigerator for 24 hours. Drain bear meat and strain and reserve the marinade. Cook bear meat in a Dutch oven in small amount of fat until browned. Sprinkle with shallots, salt, pepper and small amount of flour and add water, reserved marinade, butter, Worcestershire sauce and mushrooms. Simmer for 2 hours or until the bear meat is tender, adding water as needed. 4 servings.

Mrs. T. Walls, Autaugaville, Alabama

SQUIRREL MAISON D'ETE

4 squirrels	Flour
Lemon juice	1 pt. cream
Salt and pepper to taste	

Cut the squirrels in serving pieces. Sprinkle with lemon juice and place in a bowl. Refrigerate overnight. Wipe with a damp cloth and rub with salt and pepper. Dredge with flour and fry in small amount of fat in a skillet for about 40 minutes or until brown. Place in a casserole and add cream. Bake at 425 degrees for 20 minutes. 6 servings.

Mrs. Francis Beaulieu, Wetumpka, Alabama

SQUIRREL BRUNSWICK

10 squirrels, disjointed	2 lb. lima beans
2 No. 303 cans corn	1 c. diced celery
1/2 lb. salt pork, diced	Salt and pepper to taste
5 lb. potatoes, diced	1/4 c. Worcestershire sauce
2 qt. canned tomatoes	Flour
3 lb. onions, diced	

Place the squirrels in a large kettle with enough water to half cover and bring to a boil. Cover the kettle. Simmer until squirrels are tender and cool. Remove squirrels from stock and remove meat from bones. Place squirrels back in stock and add remaining ingredients except flour. Cook for 2 hours. Thicken with small amount of flour mixed with water and simmer for 30 minutes longer. 20 servings.

Mrs. G. E. Davis, Prattville, Alabama

RACCOON A POMME

1 raccoon, dressed	1 tsp. cinnamon
Salt and pepper to taste	1 tsp. allspice
2 peppercorns	2 tbsp. flour
2 c. dry bread cubes	4 apples, quartered
1/2 c. chopped pecans	1 tsp. brown sugar
1 c. (about) orange juice	

Place the raccoon in a Dutch oven with enough water to half cover and add the salt, pepper and peppercorns. Cook for 45 minutes to 1 hour and drain off most of the liquid. Remove raccoon from Dutch oven. Mix the bread cubes, pecans and orange juice and stuff the raccoon. Place raccoon back in the Dutch oven and sprinkle with the cinnamon, allspice and flour. Arrange the apples around raccoon and sprinkle brown sugar on apples. Bake in 350-degree oven for 45 minutes or until done. 6 servings.

Mrs. J. Paterson, Montgomery, Alabama

BAKED RATTLESNAKE

1 rattlesnake	1 tsp. basil
1 recipe thin cream sauce	1 tsp. white pepper
1/4 lb. fresh mushrooms, sliced	1 tsp. rosemary
2 limes, sliced thin	

Skin the snake, dress and wash in cold water. Cut into 3-inch sections and place in a large baking dish. Cover with cream sauce and add the mushrooms, limes, basil, pepper and rosemary. Cover tightly. Bake in 300-degree oven for 1 hour or until done. One large can sliced mushrooms may be substituted for fresh mushrooms. This recipe is from a noted hunter and storyteller. He is a great nephew of President Madison.

Richard Fleetwood Madison, Montgomery, Alabama

Kraut and Frankfurter Plank Dinner (page 154)

specialty meats

When you want to prepare a quick, inexpensive, but delicious meat course, what do you do? You turn to specialty meats, of course. These meats — canned such as corned beef, Spam or chipped beef and fresh such as liver, heart, or kidneys — are famed for their economy and nutritional value.

Canned specialty meats, when mixed with other ingredients, become stunning entrees. Perhaps the easiest to prepare and most popular specialty meat is the frankfurter, more often referred to as the hot dog.

Fun foods using specialty meats can be much more than the traditional hot dog, as the following recipes illustrate. With canned luncheon meats, you can prepare a marvelous meal in a casserole. With liver, you can create a succulent — and nutritious — liver-and-onion saute.

The possibilities of specialty meats are really endless. If the occasion calls for a lavish dish, specialty meats may be elegantly prepared. If time is short and you need an entree that is quick and easy — but nutritious — any of the canned specialty meats are ideal. And by stocking your kitchen shelf with handy canned specialty meats, you will always have an engaging entree on hand. Exciting meals are yours when you explore the wonderful world of specialty meats.

S pecialty meats include both the precooked meats available in cans from the grocer's shelf (corned beef, chipped beef, Spam, etc.) and variety meats. Because canned meats have directions for preparation right on the label, this section focuses on preparing variety meats.

Variety meats are a real bonus to the cost-conscious homemaker who wants to be sure her family is getting all the vitamins and minerals it needs. These meats — the edible organs of meat animals — include the liver, heart, kidney, tongue, tripe, brains, and sweetbreads from beef, pork, calves, or lamb. These meats are usually inexpensive and they go a long way — in most cases, a pound will yield four servings. And they are packed full of iron, vitamins A

general directions
FOR SPECIALTY MEATS

and B, and the so-called "trace minerals" so important to the human body.

In fact, these meats are so rich in needed vitamins and minerals that most home economists recommend they be served at least once a week.

Because most variety meats are delicate, they are more perishable than other meats and should be cooked and served within a day or two of their purchase. The exceptions to this rule are the smoked variety meats, such as tongue.

In cooking variety meats, as in other meats, the method used depends upon the tenderness or toughness of the meat cuts. However, because variety meats have membranes which must be softened, nearly all cuts require some form of precooking. After precooking — described below — variety meats are usually cooked by moist heat methods. Moist heat is used because of the small size of most cuts of variety meat: dry heat would evaporate the juices. The delicate flavor of variety meats may be enhanced by the careful use of a few herbs — bay leaf, celery, chive, or a light touch of garlic.

Liver is probably the favorite variety meat. It is rich in iron and is frequently recommended to cure mild forms of anemia. Veal (calf) and lamb liver are mild and tender while beef and pork are stronger in flavor and coarser in texture. It may be necessary to soak beef or pork liver in hot water for 5 minutes before cooking. Liver is usually sold presliced. Because it is a delicate meat, it should be dipped in flour before cooking. If it is not given this protective coating, liver may be dry and almost flavorless.

Kidneys are a popular variety meat and usually are served with lamb chops or in a steak-and-kidney pie. Because they are tender, lamb and veal kidneys need little cooking and may be broiled. To prepare them, remove the outer membrane and split the kidney in half. Remove the white vein and all fat, then broil according to the timetable. Follow the same procedure with beef and pork kidneys, but simmer for 30 minutes and then braise. These kidneys are too tough to be broiled.

Sweetbreads are the thymus glands of calves and lamb and are much prized for their delicate flavor and texture. They must be prepared for cooking by placing in cold water and letting stand 30 minutes. Parboil for 20 minutes in 1 quart of water with 1 teaspoon salt and 1 tablespoon vinegar. Drain, place in cold water and let set. Then remove any strings and membranes, and use as directed in the recipe.

Hearts of calves, beef, lamb, and pork are economical and very nourishing. Veal heart is the most delicate in flavor and has the tenderest texture. Hearts from all animals should be cooked slowly using moist heat. To prepare for cooking, cut out the coarse fibers on the top and inside and wash in cold water. Then place the heart in a pan, cover with water, add 1/2 to 1 teaspoon salt, and cover. Let simmer until tender — about an hour to an hour and a half per pound for veal and lamb heart, 2 hours for beef and pork heart.

Tongue comes in many forms and is a favorite served chilled and sliced. Beef tongue is most popular because it is the largest and slices best. Allow 1 pound of tongue per four servings. Cured, smoked, or pickled tongue does not need preparation before serving. Fresh tongue should be seasoned by placing it in a pan and adding 1 tablespoon salt, a small sliced onion, a few peppercorns, and a bay leaf. Cover with water and simmer 1 to 1 and 1/2 hours for lamb or veal tongue, 2 and 1/2 to 3 hours per pound for beef. Remove from heat and cool slightly. Then cut off the bone and gristle at the thick end of the tongue and peel the skin from the thick to the thin end.

Brains are similar to sweetbreads in flavor and texture, and may be used in sweetbread recipes. Brains are highly perishable and should be used immediately. To prepare them for cooking, soak in salted water (1 tablespoon salt per quart of water) for 15 minutes. Drop into boiling water and add 1 teaspoon salt. Cover and simmer 15 minutes. Drain and recover with cold water. Drain well. Use at once or keep cold in the refrigerator. If they are left in the refrigerator, the membrane should be left on.

Tripe is the muscular inner lining of the animal's stomach. It comes either in honeycomb, pocket, or plain form, but honeycomb is considered the greatest delicacy. To prepare for broiling, tripe should be placed in a pan and covered with water and 1 tablespoon salt. Cover and simmer for 1 hour.

SWEETBREADS A LA KING

1 c. chopped cooked sweetbreads	1/2 c. grated American cheese
1 can cream of chicken soup	2 tbsp. chopped pimento
1 c. milk	2 tbsp. chopped green pepper
1 tbsp. instant minced onion	1 can refrigerator biscuits

Combine all ingredients except the biscuits in a saucepan and heat over low heat for 10 to 15 minutes, stirring occasionally. Bake the biscuits according to can directions and serve sweetbread mixture over the hot biscuits. 4 servings.

Mrs. Ruth S. Allison, Manassas Park, Virginia

SKEWERED PINEAPPLE SANDWICHES

1 8 1/4-oz. can pineapple slices	8 slices salami
4 3-in. thick slices sourdough bread	8 slices mozzarella cheese
	1 egg
1/3 c. butter	1/3 c. milk
1/4 tsp. mixed Italian herbs	1/2 c. grated Parmesan cheese
Dash of garlic powder	

Preheat oven to 400 degrees. Drain the pineapple. Make 2 slits 1 inch apart in each bread slice from top to bottom, leaving bottom crust intact. Mix the butter, Italian herbs and garlic powder and spread in slits. Wrap 1 salami slice around each mozzarella cheese slice. Place 1 pineapple slice in 1 slit and 2 salami-wrapped cheese slices in the other slit in each slice of bread. Secure each sandwich with 2 bamboo skewers. Beat the egg with milk in a shallow dish and roll skewered sandwiches in ·egg mixture to lightly moisten surfaces. Place on buttered baking sheet and sprinkle with Parmesan cheese. Bake for about 15 minutes or until browned. 4 sandwiches.

Skewered Pineapple Sandwiches (above)

BARBECUED TONGUE

1 beef tongue	1 green pepper, chopped
2 cloves of garlic	1/3 c. chopped sweet pickle
2 stalks celery	1/3 c. vinegar
1 onion, sliced	1/2 c. catsup
1 tsp. peppercorns	2 tsp. sugar
1 onion, chopped	2 tsp. mustard

Place the tongue in a saucepan and cover tongue with cold water. Add the garlic, celery, onion and peppercorns. Cover and bring to a boil. Reduce heat and simmer for 3 hours. Drain and discard the broth. Remove skin and gristle from the thick end of the tongue. Slice and place in greased baking dish. Combine remaining ingredients in a saucepan and bring to a boil. Pour the sauce over the tongue, and place cover on top. Bake at 350 degrees for 30 minutes. 4 servings.

Mrs. R. J. Wayland, Mart, Texas

LIVER LOAF

1 lb. beef liver	1/8 tsp. sage
1 med. onion	1/8 tsp. thyme
3 strips bacon	1 c. soft bread crumbs
1 clove of garlic	1 egg, beaten
1 tsp. salt	1/4 c. milk or evaporated milk
1/4 tsp. pepper	1/4 c. tomato juice or catsup

Grind the liver, onion, bacon and garlic and mix well. Add the seasonings, bread crumbs, egg and milk and press into oiled loaf pan. Pour the tomato juice over the liver mixture. Bake at 350 degrees for 1 hour and 15 minutes. Serve hot with tomato sauce. 4 servings.

Mrs. Mildred Pierce, Pampa, Texas

BEEF CREOLE DINNER

1 lge. onion, chopped	1 No. 2 can corn
1 green pepper, chopped	1 No. 2 can string beans
3 tbsp. butter	1 No. 2 can tomatoes
2 eggs, beaten	1/4 tsp. chili powder
1 1-lb. can corned beef, flaked	Salt and pepper to taste
	1 c. bread crumbs

Brown the onion and green pepper in butter in a saucepan and cool. Stir in the eggs. Add the corned beef, vegetables and seasonings and cook for 10 minutes. Pour half the beef mixture into a greased casserole and add half the bread crumbs. Add remaining beef mixture and top with remaining bread crumbs. Bake at 350 degrees for 20 minutes.

Mildred Gresham, Cadiz, Kentucky

Bravo Corned Beef and Corn Bread (below)

BRAVO CORNED BEEF AND CORN BREAD

1 egg	1 tsp. salt
1/2 c. milk	1/2 tsp. oregano
1 10-oz. package easy corn bread	1/4 tsp. pepper
mix	1 tsp. cornstarch
3/4 lb. corned beef, chopped	Parmesan cheese
1 1-lb. can kidney beans	Parsley sprigs
1 1-lb. can stewed tomatoes	

Preheat oven to 425 degrees. Place the egg and milk in bag of corn bread mix. Squeeze upper part of bag to force air out and close top of bag by holding tightly between thumb and index finger. Place bag on a table and mix, working bag vigorously with fingers, for about 40 seconds or until egg is completely blended. Squeeze bag to empty batter into ungreased aluminum pan contained in package. Bake for about 20 minutes. Brown the corned beef in a skillet in a small amount of fat, then drain off excess drippings. Drain the kidney beans and add to corned beef. Add the tomatoes, 1/4 cup water, salt, oregano and pepper and cook over medium heat for 20 minutes. Mix the cornstarch with small amount of water and stir into corned beef mixture. Cook for about 5 minutes longer or until slightly thickened. Cut the corn bread into 6 pieces. Split each piece horizontally and toast. Place 2 pieces of corn bread on each serving plate and spoon corned beef mixture over corn bread. Sprinkle with Parmesan cheese and garnish with parsley. 6 servings.

DRIED BEEF SUPREME

1 sm. jar dried beef	1 can mushroom soup
2 tbsp. butter or margarine	1 sm. can mushroom pieces
1 med. green pepper, chopped	1/2 soup can milk

Cut the dried beef into small pieces. Melt the butter in a saucepan and saute the dried beef and green pepper lightly. Add the soup and mushroom pieces and stir in the milk. Heat through. May be served over toast or hot grits. 4 servings.

LAMB KIDNEYS IN RICE RING

1 1/4 c. butter or margarine	12 lamb kidneys
1/2 lb. mushrooms, sliced	1 tbsp. crushed rosemary
1 clove of garlic, crushed	3 tbsp. lemon juice
1 lge. onion, sliced	2 c. rice
1/4 tsp. salt	Chicken broth
1/8 tsp. pepper	1/2 c. finely chopped parsley

Melt 1 cup butter in a skillet. Add the mushrooms and cook over high heat until tender. Remove mushrooms from skillet and keep warm. Add the garlic, onion, salt and pepper to hot butter in skillet and cook over low heat until onion is lightly browned. Remove from skillet and keep warm. Split and trim the kidneys, add to hot skillet and sprinkle with rosemary. Cook over high heat, turning frequently, for 7 to 9 minutes or until kidneys are tender but still pink in the center. Return mushrooms and onion mixture to skillet and sprinkle with lemon juice. Cook for 5 minutes longer. Drain and reserve butter sauce. Cook the rice according to package directions, using chicken broth for liquid, then stir in remaining butter and parsley. Pack with a spoon into lightly greased 5 1/2-cup ring mold and let stand for 10 minutes. Unmold onto a serving plate and fill center with kidney mixture. Serve with reserved butter sauce. 6-8 servings.

Lamb Kidneys in Rice Ring (above)

153

SUNSHINE CASSEROLE

2 4-oz. cans Vienna sausage	1 tall can evaporated milk
3 eggs, beaten	1 tsp. salt
1 1-lb. can cream-style corn	1/4 tsp. pepper

Cut the Vienna sausage into 1/4-inch slices. Mix eggs, 2/3 of the sausage, corn, milk, salt and pepper and pour into a shallow 1 1/2-quart casserole. Place in pan of hot water. Bake in 350-degree oven for 40 to 50 minutes or until a knife inserted in center comes out clean. Place remaining sausage on top and bake for 10 minutes longer. 6 servings.

Harriet Hickman, Lenoir City, Tennessee

OXTAIL STEW WITH PARSLEY DUMPLINGS

1 2 1/2 to 3-lb. oxtail	1 1/2 tsp. celery salt
Flour	2 whole cloves
Salt and pepper	2 bay leaves
4 tbsp. fat	2 c. diced potatoes
2 1/2 c. water	2 c. sliced carrots
1 c. sliced onions	12 sm. whole onions
1 No. 2 can tomatoes	4 tsp. baking powder
1 tbsp. lemon juice	1/2 c. chopped parsley
1 clove of garlic, halved	1 1/4 c. milk
1 tsp. Worcestershire sauce	1/4 c. melted fat or oil
1 tsp. sugar	

Cut the oxtail into 1 1/2-inch lengths. Mix 1 cup flour with salt and pepper to taste and dredge the oxtail pieces in the seasoned flour. Brown in hot fat in a Dutch oven. Add the water, onions, tomatoes, lemon juice, garlic, Worcestershire sauce, sugar, celery salt, cloves, bay leaves and 1 tablespoon salt and cover. Simmer for 3 hours. Add the vegetables and simmer for 30 minutes longer or until tender. Sift 2 cups flour, 1 1/4 teaspoons salt and baking powder together into a mixing bowl. Combine the parsley, milk and melted fat and add to sifted ingredients. Stir just until blended and drop by spoonfuls into hot stew. Cover and cook for 12 minutes without lifting cover.

Mrs. M. G. Cassidy, Durham, Arkansas

KRAUT AND FRANKFURTER PLANK DINNER

1 clove of garlic, minced	8 carrots
1/2 c. chopped onion	1/4 c. (firmly packed) light
5 tbsp. butter or margarine	brown sugar
2 c. drained sauerkraut	1 tbsp. light corn syrup
3 tbsp. sugar	2 tbsp. prepared mustard
1/2 tsp. salt	8 frankfurters
Pepper to taste	Melted butter
1 4-oz. can pimentos	4 servings mashed potatoes

Saute the garlic and onion in 3 tablespoons butter in a large skillet until tender. Add the sauerkraut, sugar, 1/4 teaspoon salt and pepper. Drain the pimentos and dice. Add to sauerkraut mixture and toss until well mixed. Cover and keep warm over low heat. Pare the carrots and cut diagonally into 1-inch slices. Simmer in salted water for about 20 minutes or until tender, then drain. Combine remaining butter, brown sugar, corn syrup, mustard and remaining salt in a small saucepan and heat until blended, stirring constantly. Pour over carrots and toss gently until coated. Place the sauerkraut mixture in center of a large heatproof plank. Cut 3 diagonal slits, about 1/2 inch deep, in frankfurters and brush frankfurters with melted butter. Arrange frankfurters, slit side down, carrots and mashed potatoes around sauerkraut mixture and drizzle melted butter over potatoes. Broil 6 to 8 inches from heat until frankfurters are browned. Turn the frankfurters and brown on other side. 4 servings.

Photograph for this recipe on page 146.

MACARONI WITH FRANKFURTER SAUCE

1 tbsp. salad oil	Salt
12 frankfurters	1/8 tsp. crushed red pepper
1 c. chopped onions	1 tsp. crushed basil leaves
2 cloves of garlic, crushed	4 to 5 qt. boiling water
2 6-oz. cans tomato paste	3 c. elbow macaroni
2 beef bouillon cubes	

Heat the oil in a large skillet over medium heat. Cut the frankfurters crosswise in 1/4-inch slices and brown in the oil, small amount at a time. Remove frankfurters with slotted spoon and drain on paper toweling. Saute the onions and garlic in same skillet until tender, then stir in the tomato paste, 3 cups water, bouillon cubes, 3/4 teaspoon salt, red pepper and basil. Bring to a boil, stirring constantly, and cover. Simmer for 30 minutes. Add the frankfurters and simmer for about 15 minutes longer. Add 1 1/2 tablespoons salt to boiling water and add macaroni gradually so that water continues to boil. Cook, stirring occasionally, until tender, then drain in a colander. Place macaroni in hot serving dish and top with frankfurter sauce. Garnish with parsley, if desired. 6 servings.

Macaroni with Frankfurter Sauce (above)

Twin High Boy Krautwiches (below)

TWIN HIGH BOY KRAUTWICHES

1 5-oz. jar pasteurized process blue cheese spread	Dash of freshly ground pepper
1 12-oz. can beer	1 6-in. round loaf pumpernickel bread
2 c. well-drained sauerkraut	Lettuce
1/2 c. chopped radishes	1/2 lb. sliced cooked ham
3 tbsp. finely chopped parsley	1/2 lb. sliced cooked beef salami
1/4 tsp. seasoned salt	

Combine the blue cheese spread and 2 tablespoons beer in a bowl and mix well. Set aside. Place remaining beer and sauerkraut in a saucepan and simmer for about 5 minutes. Cool completely and drain thoroughly. Add chopped radishes, parsley, seasoned salt and pepper and toss to blend seasonings. Cut the bread horizontally into 6 slices and spread blue cheese mixture on all cut surfaces. Use 3 slices of bread for each high boy and assemble simultaneously on separate boards or plates. Score bottom and top crusts into quarters for easier cutting. Top first slice of bread for each high boy with lettuce, 1/4 of the sauerkraut mixture, 1/4 of the ham slices and 1/4 of the salami slices. Add second slice of bread and repeat lettuce, sauerkraut mixture, ham and salami layers. Top with third slice of bread and wrap. Chill for about 1 hour before serving. Cut each high boy into quarters and garnish with radish roses and pickle slices. 8 servings.

CREAMED BRAINS IN POTATO CASES

2 pr. calf brains	1 tsp. celery salt
2 c. medium white sauce	1 tsp. paprika

1 tsp. salt
Dash of Worcestershire sauce

3 c. cooked mashed potatoes
Parsley

Wash the brains and remove skin and veins. Soak in cold, salted water for 20 minutes, then drain. Place in a saucepan, cover with boiling water and simmer for 20 minutes. Drain, cool and cut into cubes. Mix with white sauce and add seasonings. Heat to boiling point. Make nests of mashed potatoes on a large, buttered platter. Fill potato nests with brains mixture and garnish with parsley.

Mrs. Flora May Miller, Elkhart, Texas

MAIN DISH NOODLE PUDDING

Salt
4 to 5 qt. boiling water
6 c. fine egg noodles
2 tbsp. salad oil
1 1/4 c. chopped onion
1/2 c. chopped parsley

1/4 tsp. freshly ground pepper
1/4 tsp. ground nutmeg
1 12-oz. can luncheon meat, diced
4 eggs
2 c. reliquified nonfat dry milk
1/3 c. grated Parmesan cheese

Add 1 1/2 tablespoons salt to boiling water and add noodles gradually so that water continues to boil. Cook, stirring occasionally, until just tender and drain in a colander. Heat the oil in a large skillet over medium heat. Add the onion and saute until golden. Stir in parsley and cook just until wilted. Remove from heat and stir in 1 1/2 teaspoons salt, pepper, nutmeg and luncheon meat. Alternate 3 layers of noodles with 3 layers of meat mixture in a buttered 2 1/2-quart casserole, beginning with noodles and ending with meat mixture. Beat the eggs, milk and cheese together in a bowl and pour over noodle mixture. Cover. Bake in 350-degree oven for 35 minutes. Uncover and bake for 20 minutes longer.

Main Dish Noodle Pudding (above)

combination meats

Recipes in the combination meats category utilize almost every mix of meats imaginable. They stretch your imagination by putting together in one recipe meats such as veal and ham. Either of these meats is normally an entree in itself. To mix meats in one recipe is to many women an unheard of idea.

Readers of *Southern Living* have learned how to combine meats successfully. They know that besides adding necessary nutrition, entrees using combination meats break with tradition by providing an unusual two-in-one approach to cooking.

Your family will marvel at your ingenuity when you use a recipe calling for combination meats. Whatever your family's food preferences, you will be able to find something to please everyone on the following pages. From tamales to applesauce meatballs, the combination meats recipes are an exciting array of food ideas.

And by using any of the recipes for combination meats, you are giving each member of your family valuable, body-building protein — the kind we all need every day.

These recipes are Southern favorites and are shared with you by readers of *Southern Living*. Some are family treasures handed from one generation to the next. All of them have been enjoyed by Southern families.

ALSATIAN CHOUCROUTE GARNIE

1/4 lb. salt pork, cut in cubes	1/2 tsp. thyme
2 med. onions, sliced	1 bay leaf
1 lb. sliced Italian sausage, halved	6 peppercorns
	6 juniper berries
1/2 lb. cooked cubed ham	1 1/2 lb. frankfurters, halved
6 1/2 c. drained sauerkraut	10 med. cooked potatoes
3 c. beef broth	2 tbsp. chopped parsley
1 tsp. salt	

Saute the salt pork in a large saucepan or Dutch oven until golden brown. Stir in the onions, sausage and ham and cook until onions are crisp-tender and sausage and ham are browned. Remove onions and meats from saucepan. Place sauerkraut in saucepan and cook, stirring, until lightly browned. Return onions and meats to saucepan and stir in the broth, salt and thyme. Tie bay leaf, peppercorns and juniper berries in a piece of cheesecloth and add to sauerkraut mixture. Cover. Simmer for 45 minutes. Stir in frankfurters and potatoes and cover. Simmer for 15 minutes longer. Arrange frankfurters and potatoes around edge of platter and pile sauerkraut mixture in center. Sprinkle potatoes with parsley. 10 servings.

Photograph for this recipe on page 158.

BEEF-NOODLE CASSEROLE

1 sm. can mushrooms	1 pt. milk
1 lb. ground round steak	1 to 2 c. sharp grated cheese
1/2 lb. ground pork	2 pkg. medium noodles
3 tbsp. bacon drippings	1 sm. can pimentos
2 tbsp. flour	1 can ripe olives

Drain the mushrooms and reserve liquid. Cook the meats in bacon drippings in a skillet until browned. Remove meats from skillet and stir the flour into the drippings. Stir in reserved mushroom liquid and milk slowly. Add the cheese and cook, stirring constantly, until thickened. Cook the noodles according to package directions and add the mushrooms, meats and chopped pimentos and olives. Place in a casserole and pour the cheese sauce over top. Bake at 350 degrees for 45 minutes to 1 hour.

Mrs. Charles R. Walston, Birmingham, Alabama

ORIENTAL SPAGHETTI

1/2 lb. spaghetti	1 15-oz. can Chinese vegetables, drained
1/2 lb. ground beef	
1/2 lb. ground pork	1 10-oz. can tomato sauce
1 c. chopped celery	1/2 tsp. salt
1/2 c. chopped onions	3/4 c. grated sharp cheese

Break up spaghetti and cook according to package directions. Brown the meats, celery and onions in a skillet, then add the Chinese vegetables, tomato sauce and salt. Mix with spaghetti. Place in a baking dish and cover with cheese. Bake for 45 minutes at 325 degrees.

Mrs. Neil A. Kain, Jr., Decatur, Georgia

LASAGNA

1/2 lb. lean ground pork	6 sprigs of parsley
1 lb. ground beef	4 tbsp. margarine
1 1/4 c. chopped onion	3 tbsp. flour
1 clove of garlic, minced	3/4 c. grated Parmesan cheese
1 lge. can tomato sauce	2 c. milk
1/2 c. water	2 egg yolks
1/4 tsp. pepper	1 pkg. lasagna
1 tsp. seasoned salt	Sliced mozzarella or Scamorzo
2 bay leaves	cheese

Place the pork and beef in a heavy skillet and cook over low heat for 15 to 20 minutes. Do not brown. Add 1 cup onion and garlic and cook over low heat until onion is tender. Add the tomato sauce, water and seasonings and simmer for about 45 minutes. Saute the remaining onion in margarine but do not brown. Mix in the flour and Parmesan cheese. Add milk slowly and cook over low heat, stirring, until sauce is thickened. Beat egg yolks slightly and add a small amount of the hot cheese mixture. Add egg yolk mixture to the cheese sauce slowly and cook for about 10 minutes, stirring constantly. Cook the lasagna according to package directions and place a layer in a greased baking dish. Add layer of tomato sauce to cover noodles, then add a layer of the cheese sauce over tomato sauce. Add a layer of mozzarella cheese. Repeat layers until all ingredients are used. Bake at 325 degrees for about 30 minutes or until bubbly and lightly browned.

Mrs. A. G. Detrich, Tyler, Texas

SAUSAGE SPAGHETTI

1 1/2 lb. ground beef	2 tsp. salt
1 lb. pork sausage	1 tsp. oregano
1 clove of garlic, minced	1/2 tsp. basil
1 c. chopped onion	1/4 tsp. chili powder
1 green pepper, chopped	2 7-oz. packages spaghetti
2 6-oz. cans tomato paste	1/2 c. sliced ripe olives
1 No. 2 1/2 can tomatoes	Grated Parmesan cheese

Place the beef, sausage, garlic, onion and green pepper in a hot skillet and cook until meats are lightly browned, stirring frequently. Pour off excess fat. Add tomato paste, tomatoes, salt, oregano, basil and chili powder to beef mixture and cover tightly. Simmer for 30 minutes. Uncover and simmer for 15 minutes longer. Cook spaghetti according to package directions and drain. Serve the meat sauce over spaghetti and sprinkle olives over sauce. Serve with cheese. 6-8 servings.

Ann Elsie Schmetzer, Madisonville, Kentucky

City Chicken with Zesty Mustard Sauce (below)

CITY CHICKEN WITH ZESTY MUSTARD SAUCE

1/2 lb. boneless veal	2 c. water
1/2 lb. boneless pork	1 tsp. Worcestershire sauce
1 1/2 tsp. salt	1 tbsp. prepared mustard
1/4 tsp. pepper	1 10-oz. package frozen peas
1/4 c. flour	1 tbsp. butter
1 lge. can evaporated milk	1 1/3 c. packaged precooked rice
3 tbsp. salad oil	

Cut the veal and pork in 1-inch cubes and place alternately on 6 skewers. Mix 1 teaspoon salt and pepper with the flour. Dip skewered meats in 1/3 cup evaporated milk, then dip in flour mixture to coat well. Reserve remaining flour mixture for gravy. Brown the meats in hot oil in a heavy saucepan. Add 1 cup water and bring to a boil. Reduce heat and cover saucepan. Simmer for about 1 hour or until meats are tender. Sprinkle reserved flour mixture over liquid around meats and blend in smoothly. Stir in remaining evaporated milk, Worcestershire sauce and mustard and cook over medium heat, stirring, until thickened. Cook the peas with butter and remaining water and salt according to package directions, then stir in rice. Cover and let stand for 5 minutes. Place in a serving dish. Place chicken on rice and pour sauce over chicken. 6 servings.

MEAT PIE

2 onions, chopped	2 c. diced cooked potatoes
1 c. chopped celery	1 c. diced cooked carrots
3/4 c. butter or meat drippings	1 c. peas (opt.)
1 lb. beef, cut in cubes	2 1/4 c. flour
1 lb. veal, cut in cubes	4 tsp. baking powder
3 tsp. salt	3 tbsp. shortening
1 tsp. pepper	3/4 c. milk

Cook the onions and celery in 1/2 cup butter in a skillet until tender. Add the meats and cook until brown. Add enough water to cover all ingredients, then add 2 teaspoons salt and pepper. Simmer until the meats are tender. Drain and reserve liquid. Add the potatoes, carrots and peas to the meat mixture and place in a greased casserole. Melt remaining butter in the skillet and stir in 1/4 cup flour. Add enough water to reserved liquid to make 4 cups liquid and stir into flour mixture. Cook, stirring constantly, until thickened, then pour over meat mixture. Combine remaining flour, baking powder and remaining salt in a mixing bowl and cut in shortening. Stir in the milk. Roll out on a floured surface and cut with a biscuit cutter. Place on meat mixture. Bake at 450 degrees for 20 minutes.

Mrs. C. B. Bushager, Del Rio, Texas

MEAT TURNOVERS

Flour	3 tbsp. chopped parsley
Shortening	Salt
2 lge. onions, diced	Pepper to taste
6 green onions, diced	2 eggs, beaten
3/4 lb. ground beef	2 tsp. baking powder
3/4 lb. ground pork	Milk

Brown 2 tablespoons flour in 1 tablespoon shortening in a skillet. Add onions and meats and cook, stirring, until brown. Add the parsley, salt to taste and pepper and let stand until cold. Melt 1/2 cup shortening and cool. Add the eggs, 4 cups flour, baking powder and 1/2 teaspoon salt, then mix in enough milk to make a stiff dough. Roll out on floured surface and cut in 6-inch circles. Place meat mixture on half of each circle and moisten edges with water. Fold over and seal with a fork. Fry in deep fat until brown. 24-28 servings.

Mrs. A. J. Redmon, Donaldsonville, Louisiana

TAMALE PIE

1/2 c. chopped onion	1 tsp. salt
1/2 clove of garlic, chopped	1 c. cornmeal
1 lb. ground beef	1/2 c. milk
1 lb. sausage	2 beaten eggs
2 cans tomato sauce	Ripe olives
1 can whole kernel corn	Grated cheese
1 tbsp. chili powder	

Saute the onion and garlic for 5 minutes. Add the beef, sausage, tomato sauce, corn and liquid, chili powder and salt and cook for 15 minutes. Add the corn-meal, milk and eggs slowly and cook for 10 minutes longer. Pour into a greased baking dish and dot with ripe olives. Bake in 325-degree oven for 55 minutes. Cover with cheese and bake for 5 minutes longer. 8 servings.

Mrs. Lena Codner, Marietta, Georgia

Party Ham Loaf with Tropical Raisin Sauce (below)

PARTY HAM LOAF WITH TROPICAL RAISIN SAUCE

3 c. cereal flakes	1 tbsp. prepared mustard
1 1/2 lb. ground smoked ham	1/2 tsp. coarsely ground pepper
1/2 lb. ground chuck	1/4 c. dark seedless raisins
3 beaten eggs	2 tbsp. (packed) brown sugar
1/2 c. water	2 tbsp. pineapple juice

Crush the cereal flakes with a rolling pin. Combine with the ham, chuck, eggs, water, mustard and pepper in a bowl and mix thoroughly. Shape into sixteen 1-inch thick patties. Stand patties on edge in 8-inch ring mold and tuck raisins between patties. Mix the brown sugar and pineapple juice and spoon over patties. Bake at 350 degrees for 1 hour. Unmold on a serving platter. 8 servings.

Tropical Raisin Sauce

1/2 c. dark seedless raisins	1 tbsp. cornstarch
1 c. pineapple juice	1 tbsp. butter or margarine
1/4 c. (packed) brown sugar	

Combine all ingredients in a saucepan and cook over low heat, stirring constantly, until clear and thickened. Spoon over Party Ham Loaf. 1 1/4 cups.

BAKED HAM LOAF

1 1/2 c. brown sugar	1 c. water
1 tbsp. dry mustard	2 lb. ground ham
1/2 c. vinegar (opt.)	1 1/2 lb. ground pork

1 c. cracker crumbs
1 c. milk
2 eggs, beaten
Salt and pepper to taste

1 onion, chopped (opt.)
1 sm. green pepper, chopped
(opt.)

Combine the brown sugar, mustard, vinegar and water in a saucepan and boil for 3 minutes. Combine remaining ingredients and mix well. Place in a loaf pan. Bake at 325 degrees for 1 hour and 30 minutes, basting occasionally with sauce. 15 servings.

Mrs. Flora Patton, McMinnville, Tennessee

GLAZED HAM LOAF

2 lb. ground smoked ham
1 lb. ground fresh ham
1 c. coarse bread crumbs
1 egg, slightly beaten
3/4 c. milk
1/8 tsp. pepper

1/2 tsp. prepared mustard
1 tbsp. vinegar
2 tsp. soft butter
1/4 c. (firmly packed)
  brown sugar
Whole cloves

Combine the smoked ham, fresh ham, bread crumbs, egg, milk, pepper, mustard and vinegar and mix well. Press into a waxed paper-lined 9 x 5 x 3-inch loaf pan. Unmold into shallow baking pan and remove paper. Mix the butter and brown sugar and spread over loaf. Stud with cloves. Bake at 375 degrees for 1 hour or until done. 12 servings.

Joyce Henson, Yazoo City, Mississippi

MERINGUE MEAT LOAF

1 1/2 lb. ground beef
1/2 lb. pork sausage
3/4 c. quick-cooking oatmeal
1 c. cracker crumbs
1 c. finely chopped onion
1 sm. clove of garlic, mashed
2 1/8 tsp. salt

1/4 tsp. chili powder
1/4 tsp. pepper
1 c. milk
2 eggs, separated
1/4 tsp. cream of tartar
1/4 c. catsup

Combine the meats with oatmeal, crumbs, onion, garlic, 2 teaspoons salt, chili powder and pepper and mix thoroughly. Add milk to slightly beaten egg yolks and blend with the meat mixture. Pack into a greased 9 1/4 x 5 1/4 x 2 3/4-inch loaf pan and chill. Unmold onto a shallow baking pan. Bake for 1 hour and 30 minutes in 350-degree oven. Remove from oven and let stand for several minutes. Add the remaining salt and cream of tartar to egg whites and beat until stiff. Fold in catsup carefully. Cover top and sides of loaf with meringue. Return to oven and bake for about 15 minutes or until golden brown. Garnish with parsley. 8 servings.

Mrs. Lenora McIntyre, Bossier City, Louisiana

VEGETABLE-MEAT LOAF

I lb. ground pork	1/2 c. chopped onion
1 lb. ground beef	1/4 c. diced celery
1 tsp. salt	1/3 c. diced carrots
1/2 tsp. pepper	2 tbsp. chopped parsley
1 tsp. curry powder	2 tbsp. shortening
2 tbsp. chili sauce	1 c. canned tomatoes

Mix the ground pork, ground beef, salt, pepper, curry powder and chili sauce in a large mixing bowl. Cook the onion, celery, carrots and parsley in shortening in a saucepan for 5 minutes, stirring frequently. Add to the meat mixture and mix well. Shape into a loaf and place in a greased baking dish. Cover with the tomatoes. Bake at 400 degrees for about 45 minutes.

Mrs. W. Q. Fowler, Knoxville, Tennessee

CRANBERRY MEAT LOAF

1/4 c. brown sugar	3/4 c. cracker crumbs
1/2 c. cranberry sauce	2 eggs, beaten
1 1/2 lb. ground beef	Salt and pepper to taste
1/2 lb. ground ham	2 tbsp. chopped onion
3/4 c. milk	3 bay leaves

Spread the sugar over bottom of a greased loaf pan. Mash cranberry sauce and spread over sugar. Combine remaining ingredients except bay leaves. Shape into loaf and place on cranberry sauce. Place bay leaves on top. Bake at 350 degrees for 1 hour. Remove bay leaves and serve. 8-10 servings.

Mrs. S. F. Haase, Houston, Texas

CONGEALED MEAT LOAF

1 lb. round steak, fat removed	1 tbsp. Durkees dressing
1 lb. pork, fat removed	1 tbsp. Worcestershire sauce
Salt to taste	1 tbsp. vinegar
1 env. unflavored gelatin	1 tbsp. French dressing
1 sm. green pepper, chopped	1 tbsp. mayonnaise
1 sm. can English peas, drained	Chopped sweet pickle to taste
2 pimentos, chopped	

Place the steak and pork in a saucepan, add salt and cover with water. Bring to a boil and simmer until tender. Drain and reserve 1 3/4 cups broth. Grind steak and pork together. Soften gelatin in 1/4 cup water. Heat the reserved broth to boiling point and stir in gelatin until dissolved. Stir in ground meats. Add remaining ingredients and mix well. Pour into a mold and chill until set.

Mrs. Zelle M. Jones, Demopolis, Alabama

CHEESE RIBBON MEAT LOAF

5 slices bread	1 1/4 tsp. salt
1 c. milk	1/4 tsp. pepper
1 egg, beaten	1 tbsp. Worcestershire sauce
1 lb. ground beef	1 egg white, slightly beaten
1/4 lb. ground pork	1 tbsp. water
1/4 c. chopped onion	1/4 lb. Cheddar cheese, grated

Tear 3 slices of bread into pieces. Add the milk, egg, meats, onion, salt, pepper and Worcestershire sauce and mix thoroughly. Press 1/2 of the mixture into loaf pan. Combine the egg white and water. Tear remaining bread into pieces and mix with the egg white mixture. Stir in the cheese and spread over meat mixture. Top with remaining meat mixture. Bake at 350 degrees for 1 hour and 30 minutes. 8 servings.

Mrs. Joyce L. Geib, Hardy, Arkansas

POTATO MEAT LOAF

4 med. potatoes, sliced	6 crackers, crumbled
1 onion, sliced	1 tsp. chili powder
1/2 lb. ground beef	1/2 tsp. salt
1/2 lb. bulk sausage	1/4 tsp. pepper
1 egg, beaten	1/2 c. Cheddar cheese soup

Place the potatoes in a baking dish and place onion over potatoes. Combine the ground beef, sausage, egg, crackers, chili powder, salt and pepper and mix well. Press into baking dish over onion and spread the soup over beef mixture. Bake for 1 hour at 350 degrees.

Rachel Keisler, Marion, North Carolina

UPSIDE-DOWN HAM LOAF

3 tbsp. margarine or butter	3/4 c. dry bread crumbs
1/2 c. brown sugar	1/3 c. milk
5 slices pineapple	3 eggs, beaten
3 1/2 c. ground ham	1/4 tsp. pepper
3/4 lb. lean ground pork	

Melt the margarine in a baking dish and sprinkle with brown sugar. Arrange pineapple slices on sugar. Mix the ham, pork, bread crumbs, milk, eggs and pepper and press into prepared baking dish. Cover baking dish. Bake at 400 degrees for 40 to 45 minutes. Reduce temperature to 300 degrees and remove cover. Bake for 20 minutes longer, cool slightly and turn out onto serving dish.

Mrs. Alvah A. Hardy, Orlando, Florida

Scandinavian Meatballs au Gratin (below)

SCANDINAVIAN MEATBALLS AU GRATIN

2 1/2 c. milk	7 tbsp. butter
3/4 c. soft bread crumbs	1 1/2 lb. lean ground beef
1 egg, beaten	1/2 lb. lean ground pork
2 1/2 tsp. salt	1/4 c. flour
1/8 tsp. pepper	1 c. shredded Cheddar cheese
1/4 tsp. nutmeg	4 c. hot cooked rice
6 tbsp. minced onion	1/4 c. chopped parsley

Mix 1/2 cup milk and bread crumbs in a mixing bowl and let stand until softened. Add the egg, 1 1/2 teaspoons salt, pepper and nutmeg and mix until well blended. Saute 1/4 cup onion in 2 tablespoons butter in a skillet until transparent and add to bread mixture. Add the meats and blend well. Shape into 1-inch balls and brown in 3 tablespoons butter in the skillet. Remove from skillet. Add the flour to skillet drippings and blend well. Add remaining milk slowly and cook, stirring constantly, until smooth and thickened. Remove from heat, add remaining salt and cheese and stir until cheese melts. Add the meatballs and heat through. Saute remaining onion in remaining butter until transparent. Add the rice and parsley and toss lightly. Press around sides of a 2 1/2-quart casserole and pour meatball mixture in center. Bake at 350 degrees for 30 minutes. 8 servings.

APPLESAUCE MEATBALLS

3/4 lb. ground beef	1/2 c. thick unsweetened
1/4 lb. ground pork	applesauce

1/2 c. (packed) soft bread
crumbs
1 egg, well beaten
1/4 c. chopped onion
1 1/4 tsp. salt
1/8 tsp. pepper
Flour
1/4 c. catsup or chili sauce
1/4 c. water

Combine the meats, applesauce, bread crumbs, egg, onion and seasonings and shape into 12 balls. Roll in flour and brown in small amount of fat in a skillet. Place the meatballs in a greased deep baking dish. Mix the catsup and water and pour over meatballs. Cover baking dish. Bake at 350 degrees for 1 hour and 15 minutes. 6 servings.

Alta Cunningham, Lonoke, Arkansas

SWEDISH HAM BALLS IN SWEET-SOUR SAUCE

1 1/2 lb. ground pork
1 lb. ground ham
2 c. cracker or bread crumbs
2 eggs, slightly beaten
1 c. milk
1/2 tsp. salt
1/2 tsp. monosodium glutamate
1 c. brown sugar
1 tsp. dry mustard
1/2 c. vinegar
1/2 c. water
1/4 c. seedless raisins

Combine first 7 ingredients in a mixing bowl and mix well. Shape into balls, using 1/4 cup ham mixture for each. Place in a shallow baking dish. Bake at 350 degrees for 10 minutes. Combine remaining ingredients in a saucepan and heat until sugar dissolves. Pour over the meatballs and bake for 1 hour longer, basting occasionally.

Mrs. R. L. Waltman, Huntsville, Alabama

AUSTRIAN HERB BURGERS

6 tbsp. butter
1 egg, separated
1 lb. ground beef
1 lb. ground pork
Grated rind of 1/2 lemon
1/2 tsp. pepper
1 c. bread crumbs
Milk
2 tbsp. chopped parsley
3 tbsp. chopped onion
Juice of 1/2 lemon
1/4 c. white wine

Cream 2 tablespoons butter and stir in the egg yolk. Add the meats, lemon rind and pepper. Soak the bread crumbs in small amount of milk, then mix with the meat mixture. Fold in the stiffly beaten egg white and shape into 3/4-inch thick patties. Chill for 30 minutes. Melt remaining butter in a skillet. Add the parsley and onion and cook until golden brown, stirring constantly. Place patties in the skillet and brown on both sides over high heat. Reduce heat and add the lemon juice and wine. Cook over low heat for 5 minutes. Place patties on a hot platter and serve the sauce separately. 6 servings.

Mrs. J. Brooks, Raleigh, North Carolina

HOT TAMALES

1 lb. ground beef	4 tbsp. salt
4 tbsp. chili powder	6 c. cornmeal
1/2 lb. sausage	1 c. shortening

Combine the ground beef, chili powder, sausage and 1 tablespoon salt in a large bowl and set aside. Mix the cornmeal, remaining salt and shortening in a mixing bowl and stir in enough boiling water to hold ingredients together. Place 1 heaping tablespoon cornmeal mixture on a dampened butter paper or clean corn shuck and pat out to desired length. Place 1 tablespoon meat mixture in center of cornmeal patty and pull up paper on both sides to shape. Press edges of cornmeal patty together and pinch ends to seal. Tie ends and center of paper together with twine. Repeat with remaining cornmeal mixture and meat mixture. Place tamales in a large saucepan and cover with water. Bring to a boil, reduce heat and simmer for 40 minutes. Tamales may be frozen. 25 tamales.

Mrs. J. W. Williams, Concord, Tennessee

BEEF AND CABBAGE ROLLS

1 lb. ground beef	1/2 c. rice
1/2 lb. ground pork	1 cabbage
Salt and pepper to taste	3 c. tomato sauce
1/2 c. grated onion	2 tbsp. Worcestershire sauce

Combine the meats, salt, pepper, onion and rice and shape into rolls. Remove the core from cabbage, place cabbage in 1-quart boiling water in a saucepan and steam until leaves begin to wilt. Separate cabbage leaves and wrap each meat roll with a cabbage leaf. Secure with toothpicks and place in a casserole. Combine the tomato sauce, salt, pepper and Worcestershire sauce and pour over cabbage rolls. Cover casserole. Bake at 350 degrees for 1 hour and 30 minutes or until the rice is done. 10 servings.

Mrs. Alfred Miller, Jr., Reserve, Louisiana

VEAL CORDON BLEU

12 thin slices veal	2 eggs, beaten
Salt	1/4 c. oil
Pepper	2 tbsp. butter
6 slices Swiss cheese	1 c. chicken stock
6 slices boiled ham	1 tsp. tomato paste
1/2 c. bread crumbs	1/2 c. Marsala or sweet wine
1/2 c. flour	1 tbsp. cornstarch
Paprika	

Pound the veal until flattened and season with salt and pepper to taste. Place 1 slice each of cheese and ham on 6 slices veal and cover each slice of ham with remaining slices of veal. Mix the bread crumbs and flour with salt, pepper and paprika to taste and dip each veal sandwich into crumb mixture. Reserve remaining crumb mixture. Place veal sandwiches on a platter and refrigerate overnight. Mix eggs with 4 tablespoons water and 1/2 teaspoon salt. Place oil and butter in a skillet and heat. Dip veal sandwiches in reserved crumb mixture, dip in egg mixture, then dip in crumb mixture again. Brown on both sides in hot oil mixture and place in a shallow baking pan. Bake in preheated 375-degree oven for 15 minutes. Combine the chicken stock, tomato paste and Marsala in a saucepan and bring to a boil. Reduce heat. Mix the cornstarch with 2 tablespoons water and stir into the chicken stock mixture. Cook until thickened, stirring constantly, and serve over veal mixture. 6 servings.

Mrs. James Weil Lederer, Greensboro, North Carolina

PONDEROSA BEEF ROLLS

3 slices boiled ham, halved	1/2 tsp. salt
6 slices beef round, pounded thin	1/2 tsp. chili powder
Pepper to taste	1/4 tsp. basil
3 tbsp. butter	1/3 c. smooth peanut butter
1 med. onion, chopped	1/2 green pepper, sliced
1 clove of garlic, minced	1/3 c. sliced stuffed olives
1 c. tomato juice	Hot cooked rice

Place 1/2 ham slice on each beef slice and sprinkle with pepper. Roll up and secure with toothpicks or string. Brown in butter in a large skillet and pour off excess drippings. Stir in onion, garlic, tomato juice, salt, chili powder and basil and cover skillet. Simmer for 1 hour. Spread peanut butter over beef rolls and add green pepper and olives. Cook for 30 minutes longer or until beef is tender, stirring occasionally. Place beef rolls in a serving dish and pour sauce over rolls. Border dish with rice.

Ponderosa Beef Rolls (above)

171

EMPANADAS

1 lb. hamburger, crumbled	2 slices bread, crumbled
1/2 lb. sausage, crumbled	1/2 can tomato paste
1 lge. onion, chopped	1 1/2 c. water
2 cloves of garlic, chopped	2 recipes pastry for 2-crust
1 tsp. chili powder	pies
Salt to taste	Melted butter

Cook the hamburger, sausage, onion and garlic in a large skillet until brown, stirring frequently. Add the chili powder, salt, bread, tomato paste and water and mix well. Cook over low heat until thickened. Roll out the pastry on a floured surface and cut into 6-inch circles. Place the meat mixture on half the circles, fold over and crimp the edges with a fork. Brush with butter and place on a baking sheet. Bake at 350 degrees until brown.

Mrs. Hope Livingston, Little Rock, Arkansas

BARBECUED BURGERS

1 lge. onion, chopped	1 can corned beef, diced
1 lb. ground beef	1/2 bottle barbecue sauce
Salt to taste	

Saute the onion in a skillet until tender. Add the ground beef, salt and corned beef and cook until meats are brown. Add the barbecue sauce. Simmer for 10 to 15 minutes, then serve in hot buns.

Mrs. James R. Wilson, Prattville, Alabama

SAUCISSE BEEFBALLS

1 lb. ground beef	1 egg, beaten
1/4 lb. bulk pork sausage	1 1/2 tsp. salt
1 sm. onion, chopped	1/4 tsp. pepper
1/2 c. rice	1 can mushroom soup
1/2 c. saltine cracker crumbs	1 soup can water

Combine the beef, sausage, onion, rice, cracker crumbs, egg and seasonings and mix well. Shape into small balls and place in a well-greased 2 1/2-quart casserole. Combine the soup with water, mix well and pour over the meatballs. Bake at 375 degrees for about 1 hour or until the meatballs are tender.

Mrs. Guy M. Hogan, Atlanta, Georgia

TENDERLOIN SALAD

1 lb. beef tenderloin	1/4 c. diced olives
1 lb. lean veal	3/4 lb. brick cheese, diced
1 c. diced celery	Mayonnaise

Place the meats in a saucepan and cover with water. Bring to boiling point, then simmer until tender. Drain, cool and dice meats. Add the celery, olives and cheese and mix well. Add enough mayonnaise to moisten, then chill. Serve on lettuce. 12 servings.

Mrs. Russell Blankenship, Huntington, West Virginia

LIVER IN BAKED ONIONS

1/2 lb. calf liver	Celery salt to taste
10 slices bacon	Minced onion to taste
1 c. chopped celery	6 to 8 med. onions
1/2 tsp. salt	Buttered bread crumbs
Paprika to taste	

Scald the liver in boiling water for about 2 minutes and drain. Remove skin and grind through food chopper. Cut the bacon into small pieces and fry in a skillet until crisp. Add liver, celery and seasonings and mix well. Remove outer skin of onions, then remove centers leaving firm shell. Fill with liver mixture and sprinkle top with bread crumbs. Place in a baking pan and add small amount of water. Bake for about 1 hour at 300 degrees.

Mary Ruth Norris, Brookston, Texas

LIVER SAUSAGE

3 1/2 lb. pork	1 sm. onion, chopped (opt.)
2 lb. pork liver	Salt, pepper and sage to taste

Place the pork in a saucepan and cover with water. Bring to a boil, then simmer until tender. Drain and reserve liquid. Grind the pork and pork liver through a food chopper. Add the onion, salt, pepper, sage and enough reserved liquid to moisten and mix well. Place in molds, cover with foil and tie securely. Place on rack in a kettle with 2 inches of boiling water and cover kettle. Steam until done.

Mrs. Roxie Claborn, Albany, Kentucky

PICCADILLA

1/2 lb. ground pork	3 or 4 cloves of garlic,
2 lb. ground beef	minced
2 med. onions, chopped	1 lge. can tomatoes
1 sm. green pepper, chopped	Salt and pepper to taste
1 can tomato paste	1 bottle stuffed olives, halved

Brown the ground pork and ground beef in a skillet. Add the onions, green pepper, garlic, tomato paste, tomatoes, salt and pepper and cover. Cook over low heat for about 30 minutes. Add the olives and cover. Simmer for at least 1 hour, adding water if necessary. Serve over rice with fried bananas as accompaniment.

Mrs. J. V. Gist, Young Harris, Georgia

sauces & marinades

Many Southerners have probably heard the old argument that meat doesn't need a sauce or marinade. Good meat, so the argument goes, has its own flavor which doesn't need to be overtaken by adding fancy adornments.

People who use this argument, though, miss the point. Sauces and marinades are not designed to destroy any of the meat's distinctive flavor. Instead, by using a sauce or a marinade, the natural taste of meat is complemented.

Sauces and marinades are as varied as they are complementary. A cranberry-orange sauce for game and a rich mushroom sauce for cutlets are featured in recipes on the following pages. They illustrate the fact that a sauce for every type of meat entree may be found.

Marinades are popular in the South because a large amount of outdoor cooking is done in the region. Whether you are cooking an expensive steak, kabob or hamburger, a tangy marinade can give your meat an extra dimension.

If your family is wary of meat leftovers, give them a sauce for variety. For example, cold baked ham becomes a taste sensation when a rich peach sauce is added to it.

Used properly, sauces and marinades will complement your meat entrees. They will not change the flavor of your favorite meat but will enhance it.

There is a fine art to using sauces and marinades, an art which requires knowledge of herbs as well. But it is well worth mastering. Nothing can bring out the full flavor of meat like the perfect marinade. And nothing will complement that flavor like a delicious sauce.

Sauces may be hot or cold. Cold sauces are most often prepared with a base of French dressing, mayonnaise, or a sauce similarly rich in fat. Exceptions are cranberry, applesauce, and a few others which offer a fruit flavor to complement the meat course.

Hot sauces are infinitely more complex and it is here that the art involved in sauce-making becomes apparent. The excellence of any sauce depends on its combination of flavors. Slow cooking over very low heat allows the flavors to

general directions
FOR SAUCES AND MARINADES

mingle. Tart and spicy-flavored sauces are favorites with ham and pork. And curry is always pleasant with veal.

The most basic hot sauce is the white sauce. In a white sauce, equal parts of flour and fat are combined, cooked and then liquid and seasonings are added. The flour-and-fat mixture is called a "roux." Most American cooks make a roux by melting fat, adding flour, and adding the liquid as soon as the roux bubbles. The French prefer to let the roux cook for five minutes while they stir it constantly. The French method will take away the sometimes raw taste of cooked flour which may detract from the goodness of the sauce.

White sauce has an almost endless number of variations. To make caper sauce, add two to four tablespoons of chopped capers. To make cheese sauce, add two to four ounces of grated cheese just after the sauce has thickened. This is a good way to use up cheese that may have hardened in the refrigerator.

With imagination and a dash of this and that, the infinite variety of white sauces will add delightful taste treats to every meat course.

As sauces add zest to meat courses, so marinades add a delightful fillip of flavor. A marinade is an acid-and-oil mixture used to flavor bland meat or to tenderize the more sinewy cuts of meat. Because marinades do have acid in their base, meat should be marinated in glass or stainless steel dishes. Otherwise, the acid may affect the dish — and the flavor of the meat.

Marinades may be either cooked or uncooked. Meat will absorb flavors from cooked marinades more rapidly than from uncooked ones. If the marinating time exceeds about 12 hours, most home economists recommend using a cooked marinade. Whenever meat is to be marinated more than one hour, it should be placed in its dish, covered with the marinade and a cover of foil or waxed paper, and placed in the refrigerator. Meat cannot stay at room temperature more than an hour as bacterial activity may start.

As a general rule, cubed meat properly marinates in three to five hours. A large piece of meat marinates overnight. Marinating times should be carefully calculated: overly long marination may kill the original flavor of the meat.

A key to the fine art of sauces and marinades is careful and knowledgeable use of herbs. For a beginner, two or three basic herbs — marjoram, sage, or thyme — may be used. As you gain proficiency with these, experiment with others.

In cooking, test a very small amount of any herb, then add more as taste dictates. Use about 1/4 teaspoon of dried herbs for a meat dish to serve four. Never use more than 1/2 teaspoon. Dried herb leaves are usually four times stronger than the same measure of fresh herbs. And powdered herbs are twice as strong as dried ones.

Pure herbs and spices — not blended in mixes or prepared sauces — can often add needed flavor to salt-free diets. The only exceptions would be celery and parsley flakes which contain too much sodium.

To spark up beef stew, try a pinch (always a pinch!) of allspice. Cinnamon and cloves will turn an ordinary pot roast into a spiced gourmet delight. Chives give a mild onion flavor to soups, stews, ground meat, leftovers, and pot roasts.

Basil is delightful with any pork dish, especially those dishes which use tomatoes. Curry will give pork a deliciously oriental flavor. Mustard will add a sharply-flavorful note to ham and pork glazes. For a fabulously delicious pork stuffing, replace the usual poultry seasoning with sage, basil and savory.

Herbs must be used especially carefully with lamb because of its very delicate flavor. Chervil is delightful on broiled chops or any other cooked lamb — it should be added after cooking. Celery leaves is another favorite herb with lamb. For a different roast leg of lamb, jab the roast twice with a knife and stuff the two pockets with 1/8 teaspoon of rosemary.

With delicately-flavored veal, oregano and marjoram are two all-time favorite herbs. A combination of rosemary before cooking and savory after gives veal a tantalizing flavor.

Generally only one dish with herbs should be served at a meal — more than one will have herb flavors competing with each other.

But the careful use of herbs in sauces and marinades will pay dividends in good eating and in economy. Herbs, sauces, and marinades can make the most inexpensive cuts of meat taste like expensive roasts, chops, and steaks.

RAISIN-ORANGE SAUCE

1/4 c. finely chopped onion
1/4 c. finely chopped celery
1 c. orange juice
2 tbsp. wine vinegar

1 No. 2 can raisin pie filling
1/2 tsp. dry mustard
1/4 tsp. salt

Combine the onion, celery, orange juice and vinegar in a saucepan and mix well. Simmer until the vegetables are tender. Add remaining ingredients and heat through. Serve with ham, pork or chicken. 2 1/2 cups.

Photograph for this recipe on page 174.

FRUIT SAUCE

1   1-lb. can whole cranberry
      sauce
1/4 c. melted butter or
      margarine
2 tsp. grated orange rind

1/4 c. concentrated frozen
      orange juice
Pinch of rosemary
Salt to taste

Place all ingredients in a saucepan and mix well. Cook over low heat until heated through, stirring occasionally. Serve with pork or game. 6 servings.

Ann Elsie Schmetzer, Madisonville, Kentucky

HOT AND SPICY HAM SAUCE

1 jar pineapple preserves
1 jar apple jelly

1/2 jar horseradish
1/2 box dry mustard

Combine all ingredients in a mixing bowl and mix well. Chill overnight.

Mrs. Jeanette Boone, Hernando, Mississippi

CRANBERRY-ORANGE SAUCE

1 lb. fresh cranberries
2 c. sugar

1/2 c. orange juice
1/8 tsp. salt

Wash and pick over the cranberries. Place in a saucepan with sugar, orange juice and salt and mix well. Bring to a boil, then cover. Reduce heat and simmer until cranberry skins pop. Serve warm with game. 3 1/2 cups.

Katherine McAllister, Ferriday, Louisiana

PEACH SAUCE FOR COLD HAM

1/2 c. peach juice
3 egg yolks
Pinch of salt

1 c. finely diced peaches
1 tbsp. sherry flavoring

Heat the peach juice in a saucepan. Beat the egg yolks with salt in top of a double boiler until lemon colored, then stir in the peach juice slowly. Cook over hot water, stirring constantly, until thick and smooth. Add the peaches and sherry flavoring and refrigerate until chilled.

Janie Black, Fayetteville, North Carolina

RAISIN SAUCE

1/2 c. seedless raisins	1 tbsp. cornstarch
1/4 c. chopped citron (opt.)	1 tbsp. butter
1 c. boiling water	1/2 tsp. lemon juice
3/4 c. sugar	

Combine the raisins, citron and water in a saucepan and bring to a boil. Reduce heat and simmer for about 1 hour or until raisins are tender. Mix the sugar and cornstarch and stir into the raisin mixture. Cook, stirring constantly, for 10 minutes. Remove from heat and add butter and lemon juice. Serve over boiled ham, lamb or pork.

Mrs. Phil Ingle, Granite Falls, North Carolina

SPEEDY-DO CHERRY SAUCE

1 No. 2 can cherry pie filling	1 1/2 tsp. horseradish
2 tsp. vinegar	1/4 tsp. dry mustard

Combine the pie filling, vinegar, horseradish and mustard in a saucepan and mix well. Heat through. Serve with ham or lamb.

Speedy-Do Cherry Sauce (above)

CAPER SAUCE FOR HAM

2 tbsp. margarine	1/8 tsp. pepper
1 tbsp. flour	Dash of paprika
1 c. milk	1 tbsp. capers
1/4 tsp. salt	

Melt the margarine in a saucepan and stir in the flour until blended. Add the milk, small amount at a time, stirring constantly. Cook over medium heat, stirring, until thick and add remaining ingredients.

Mrs. Wilbur C. Johnson, Warrenton, Georgia

WINE SAUCE FOR HAM

1 c. currant jelly	4 tbsp. sugar
1 c. sweet red wine	

Combine all ingredients in a saucepan and bring to a boil over medium heat, stirring constantly. Cook until thick and serve over slices of ham. Boysenberry, loganberry or raspberry jelly may be substituted for currant jelly, if desired. 2 cups.

Mrs. R. H. Carter, Wetumpka, Alabama

HORSERADISH SAUCE

6 tbsp. butter or margarine	1 c. sour cream
6 tbsp. flour	1/4 c. prepared horseradish
3 c. beef stock	

Melt the butter in a saucepan and blend in flour. Add the stock and cook over medium heat, stirring constantly, until smooth and thickened. Remove from heat and stir in the sour cream and horseradish.

Wanda M. Argo, Knoxville, Tennessee

BUTTERMILK SAUCE

1/4 c. butter	1 tsp. salt
1 tbsp. bacon fat	1/8 tsp. pepper
1/4 c. flour	2 1/4 c. buttermilk
1 tsp. sugar	1 egg, well beaten
1 1/2 tbsp. dry mustard	

Melt the butter and bacon fat in a skillet. Mix the flour, sugar, mustard, salt and pepper and stir into the butter mixture. Add the buttermilk slowly and cook over low heat, stirring constantly, until smooth and thickened. Stir some of the hot sauce into the egg. Stir back into the sauce and cook for 3 minutes longer. Serve with game or beef.

Mrs. Will D. Martin, South Pittsburg, Tennessee

Clockwise: *Pimento-Mushroom Sauce (below), Wine Barbecue Sauce (page 185), Sour Cream and Relish Sauce (below)*

SOUR CREAM AND RELISH SAUCE

1 c. sour cream	1/2 tsp. celery salt
1/3 c. sweet pickle relish	1/8 tsp. pepper

Combine all ingredients in a bowl and mix well. Serve with hamburgers. 1 1/3 cups.

PIMENTO-MUSHROOM SAUCE

1 can cream of mushroom soup	1 c. sour cream
1/4 c. milk	1/4 c. chopped pimento

Mix all ingredients in a saucepan and cook over low heat, stirring, until heated through. Serve over cold meats.

Frankie Hutchens, Wagoner, Oklahoma

MUSHROOM-BURGUNDY SAUCE

1 can mushroom soup	1 tbsp. cornstarch
1/2 c. milk	1/2 c. red Burgundy
1 sm. can mushrooms	

Mix the soup and milk in a saucepan. Drain the mushrooms and reserve liquid. Add enough water to reserved liquid to make 1/2 cup liquid and stir into the soup mixture. Bring to a boil, stirring constantly. Mix the cornstarch with 1 tablespoon water and stir into soup mixture. Add the Burgundy and cook, stirring, until thickened. Serve with beef or pork.

Mrs. O. C. McMahorn, Columbia, Tennessee

SAUCE FOR RED MEATS

1/2 c. vinegar	Salt to taste
1/2 c. sugar	3 egg yolks, well beaten
4 tbsp. dry mustard	1 pt. cream

Combine the vinegar, sugar, mustard and salt in a saucepan and mix well. Bring to a boil and stir into the egg yolks slowly. Return to saucepan and add cream. Cook over low heat until thickened, stirring constantly.

Mrs. Earnest Johnson, Jacksonville, Alabama

HERB SAUCE

1 stick margarine or butter	1/2 tsp. basil
2 tbsp. flour	2 tbsp. minced parsley
2 c. milk	1/2 tsp. marjoram
2 tbsp. minced chives	Salt and pepper to taste

Melt the margarine in a saucepan and stir in the flour. Add the milk gradually and cook, stirring, until thickened. Add the herbs, salt and pepper. May serve with sliced tongue or veal. 6 servings.

Bess Turner, Tulsa, Oklahoma

RICH MUSHROOM SAUCE

4 tbsp. margarine	1 tsp. lemon juice
5 tbsp. flour	1/2 lb. sauteed mushrooms
2 c. beef stock	2 egg yolks, well beaten
Salt and pepper to taste	1/4 c. thick cream
1 tbsp. chopped parsley	

Melt the margarine in a saucepan and stir in the flour. Stir in the beef stock slowly and cook, stirring constantly, until thickened. Add the salt, pepper, parsley, lemon juice and mushrooms and stir well. Mix the egg yolks with cream. Stir small amount of sauce into the egg yolk mixture, then stir back into the sauce. Cook until thick, stirring constantly. Serve with veal, beefsteak or meat loaf.

Mrs. Paul Priest, Dumas, Arkansas

SIMPLE MUSHROOM SAUCE

3 tbsp. melted butter	1 can mushroom soup
3 tbsp. flour	Milk
3/4 tsp. salt	

Melt the butter in a saucepan and blend in the flour and salt. Mix the soup with enough milk to make 3 cups liquid and stir into flour mixture. Bring to boiling point, stirring, and simmer for 3 minutes. Serve with meatballs or meat patties.

Mrs. Tom B. Coleman, North Little Rock, Arkansas

BROWN SUGAR SAUCE

3/4 c. brown sugar
1/2 c. vinegar

1/2 c. water
1 tbsp. prepared mustard

Combine all ingredients in a saucepan and bring to a boil. Remove from heat and serve over frankfurters. Frankfurters may be broiled with sauce, if desired.

Mrs. E. Chamberlain, Lubbock, Texas

TOMATO-SWEET PEPPER SAUCE

2 tbsp. shortening
1 can tomatoes
1 c. water

Salt and pepper to taste
1/4 c. chopped onion
1/4 c. diced green peppers

Melt the shortening in a saucepan. Add the tomatoes, water, salt and pepper and bring to a boil. Add the onion and green peppers and cook over medium heat for about 1 hour.

Christine Angelloz, Rosedale, Louisiana

SAVORY SAUCE

1 tbsp. butter
2 tbsp. flour
1/2 tsp. salt
Dash of pepper
1/2 tsp. monosodium glutamate
1   10 3/4-oz. can beef gravy

2 tbsp. orange juice
2 tbsp. currant jelly
1   3 1/2-oz. can sliced broiled
    mushrooms
2 tbsp. sliced stuffed olives
1 bay leaf

Melt the butter in a skillet and stir in the flour, salt, pepper and monosodium glutamate. Add the gravy, orange juice and currant jelly and stir until mixed. Bring to a boil rapidly and stir in mushrooms, olives and bay leaf. Reduce heat and cover. Simmer for 30 minutes, stirring frequently and adding water, if necessary. Remove bay leaf and serve with beef roasts or patties.

Mrs. Myrtle Miller Garth, Florence, Alabama

SPICY DARK SAUCE

2 tbsp. flour
1/2 tsp. ground cloves
1 1/2 tsp. salt
1/8 tsp. pepper
2 tsp. brown sugar
1 tsp. prepared mustard

1/2 c. vinegar
3/4 c. water
1 1/2 c. catsup
2 tsp. Worcestershire sauce
1/3 c. chopped onion

Combine the flour, cloves, salt, pepper and brown sugar in a saucepan. Add remaining ingredients and mix well. Simmer for 15 minutes. 3 cups.

Isabelle Humphries, Notasulga, Alabama

Oil and Vinegar Marinade (below)

OIL AND VINEGAR MARINADE

1/2 c. corn oil	1/2 tsp. salt
1/3 c. wine vinegar	1/4 tsp. pepper
1 clove of garlic, halved	

Place all ingredients in a jar and cover. Shake well, then chill. Shake well before using. 3/4 cup.

ARABIAN SAUCE SUPREME

2 tart apples	1 tsp. ginger
1/2 c. butter or margarine	3 c. chicken stock
1 clove of garlic, minced	1 pkg. onion soup mix
2 c. chopped celery	1/4 c. flour
1 tbsp. brown sugar	2/3 c. cold water
2 tbsp. curry powder	1 c. fresh coconut milk
1/4 tsp. pepper	2 c. light cream

Peel the apples and chop. Melt the butter in a large saucepan. Add the garlic, apples and celery and cook until tender. Stir in the brown sugar, curry powder, pepper and ginger and simmer for 5 to 10 minutes. Add the chicken stock and soup mix and cover. Simmer for 25 minutes. Mix the flour with water and stir into the sauce. Add the coconut milk and cover. Simmer for 30 minutes. Add the cream and heat through. Serve with hot lamb or veal and rice. 12 servings.

Mrs. Johnnie P. Bradshaw, Ozark, Alabama

BARBECUE SAUCE

1 stick margarine	1 tbsp. Worcestershire sauce
1 lge. onion, chopped	1/3 c. vinegar
2 cloves of garlic, minced	1 c. water
1 14-oz. bottle catsup	1/4 tsp. salt
1 tsp. chili powder	1/4 tsp. pepper
2 tbsp. brown sugar	1/2 c. cola beverage or beer

Melt the margarine in a saucepan, add the onion and garlic and cook over low heat for about 5 minutes. Add the remaining ingredients except cola beverage and simmer for 30 minutes. Add cola beverage and simmer for about 15 minutes. Remove from heat and use for barbecuing pork or beef.

Mrs. R. V. Dillard, Samson, Alabama

THREE-MINUTE BARBECUE SAUCE

2 cans tomato sauce	2 tbsp. vinegar
1 env. French salad dressing	2 tbsp. salad oil
mix	1 tbsp. sugar
1 tsp. mustard	

Combine all ingredients in a small saucepan and mix well. Simmer for 3 minutes, stirring occasionally. Serve with barbecued steaks or meatballs. 2 cups.

Mrs. Sue White, Aberdeen, Maryland

WINE BARBECUE SAUCE

1/3 c. salad oil	1/2 tsp. pepper
1 clove of garlic, crushed	1/2 tsp. marjoram
2 tbsp. grated onion	1/2 tsp. thyme
1/2 tsp. salt	1/2 c. dry red wine

Combine all ingredients in a jar and cover. Shake well and let stand for 2 hours. Shake before using. Serve on beef or game.

Photograph for this recipe on page 181.

FRANCES' MEAT SAUCE

1 sm. onion, finely chopped	1 tbsp. vinegar
2 tbsp. bacon drippings	3 tbsp. lemon juice
1 tbsp. Worcestershire sauce	2 tbsp. prepared mustard
2/3 c. catsup	1 c. beef or pork broth

Fry the onion in bacon drippings in a saucepan until soft. Add remaining ingredients and simmer for 15 minutes or until thick. Serve hot on roasted meats.

Mrs. Abb McKnight, Campbellsville, Kentucky

ITALIAN SAUCE

1 med. green pepper, chopped	1/2 tsp. pepper
2 med. onions, chopped	1 tbsp. sugar
1 clove of garlic, minced	1/8 tsp. mace
1/4 c. corn oil	Dash of cayenne pepper
1 1-lb. 4-oz. can tomatoes	6 whole cloves
1 6-oz. can tomato paste	1 bay leaf
1 c. water	6 peppercorns
1 tbsp. salt	

Cook the green pepper, onions and garlic in corn oil in a heavy kettle over moderate heat for 30 minutes, stirring frequently. Add the tomatoes, tomato paste, water, salt, pepper, sugar, mace and cayenne pepper and stir well. Tie the cloves, bay leaf and peppercorns in a cheesecloth bag and add to onion mixture. Cook over low heat for 1 hour and 30 minutes, stirring occasionally. Remove cheesecloth bag and serve sauce hot over meats with spaghetti. 6 cups.

Mrs. Rozanna Menchi, Orlando, Florida

SOY SIRLOIN MARINADE

Garlic powder to taste	Meat tenderizer (opt.)
Dash of monosodium glutamate	2 c. soy sauce
Pepper to taste	2 c. water

Rub steak with first 4 ingredients. Combine soy sauce and water, add steak and marinate in refrigerator overnight. Cook steak as desired.

Mrs. Carol Scott, Hickory Flats, Mississippi

KABOBS MARINADE

1 tbsp. lemon juice	1 tsp. water
3 tbsp. salad oil	Dash of pepper
1 clove of garlic, crushed	Dash of monosodium glutamate
1/4 tsp. salt	

Combine the lemon juice, salad oil, garlic, salt, water, pepper and monosodium glutamate and pour over kabobs. Refrigerate for several hours. Cook kabobs as desired.

Barbara Schilde, Hahnville, Louisiana

MARINADE FOR STEAKS

4 tbsp. shoyu sauce	1 1/2 tbsp. sugar
4 tbsp. water	2 or 3 onions, sliced
4 tbsp. salad oil	3 tbsp. shortening
2 tsp. ground ginger	

Combine the shoyu sauce, water, oil, ginger and sugar in a bowl and mix well. Marinate steaks in sauce for 2 hours, turning occasionally. Broil steaks to desired doneness. Cook the onions in shortening in hot skillet until wilted. Add the marinade and cook until onions are tender. Serve over steaks.

Mrs. Bob Class, Pensacola, Florida

BEEF WINE MARINADE

1/4 c. salad oil	1 clove of garlic, minced
1/4 c. dry vermouth	1/4 tsp. pepper
1/4 c. soy sauce	1/2 tsp. salt
1 tsp. prepared mustard	2 tsp. Worcestershire sauce
1/2 tsp. dry mustard	

Place all ingredients in a blender container and blend for 3 minutes. Pour into a shallow pan, place steaks in marinade and refrigerate for desired length of time, turning steaks frequently.

Mrs. A. W. Herbert, Atlanta, Georgia

TARRAGON STEAK MARINADE

1 lge. onion, sliced	Salt and pepper to taste
1 lemon, cut in thin slices	1 c. oil
5 garlic cloves, pressed	3 tbsp. tarragon vinegar
1 bay leaf, crumbled	1/2 c. dry red wine
1/2 tsp. dry mustard	

Line a shallow baking dish with half the onion slices, squeeze lemon juice over onion and place lemon rinds over onion. Add half the garlic, then add bay leaf, mustard, salt and pepper. Pour in oil, vinegar and wine and place steaks on top. Place remaining onion slices on the steaks and add remaining garlic. Sprinkle with salt and pepper. Cook steaks as desired and serve the marinated onions with the steaks.

Mrs. Raymond Scott, Goldsboro, North Carolina

MARINADE FOR RED MEAT

1 c. salad oil	Dash of cayenne pepper
1/2 c. vinegar	Dash of hot sauce
2 tsp. Worcestershire sauce	2 tsp. dry mustard
1 tsp. salt	1 clove of garlic (opt.)
1/4 tsp. pepper	

Place all ingredients in a jar, cover and shake well. Remove the garlic. Place meat in marinade and refrigerate for at least 3 hours before cooking meat.

Mrs. Charles Quinn, Opp, Alabama

STEAK MARINADE

1 can onion soup	1 lge. bottle soy sauce
1 can beef broth	1 tsp. dry mustard
1 can pineapple juice	Garlic salt to taste
Juice of 1 lemon	1 tbsp. Worcestershire sauce

Combine all ingredients in a large saucepan and bring to a boil. Simmer for 5 minutes and cool. Pour over steak and marinate for about 6 hours. Cook steak as desired.

Mrs. J. R. Shea, Cherry Point, North Carolina

MARINADE FOR RABBIT

1 1/2 c. salad oil	1 tbsp. chopped green pepper
1/2 c. soy sauce	1/2 c. wine vinegar
1/4 c. Worcestershire sauce	1 1/2 tsp. dried parsley flakes
2 tbsp. dry mustard	2 cloves of garlic, crushed
Salt to taste	1/3 c. lemon juice

Combine all ingredients and mix well. Pour over rabbit and marinate for 6 hours. Cook rabbit as desired. May be used as a marinade for kabobs. 3 1/2 cups.

Mrs. J. H. Tinsley, Parris Island, South Carolina

TERIYAKI STEAK MARINADE

1/2 c. soy sauce	1/4 c. catsup
1/2 c. brandy	1 tbsp. mustard
1 1-in. piece of gingerroot, minced	1 tsp. Worcestershire sauce
	1/4 c. brown sugar

Mix all ingredients well and use as marinade for steaks.

Mrs. William Wright, Springville, Alabama

LAMB ROAST GLAZE

1/4 c. honey	1/4 tsp. ginger
1/4 c. pineapple juice	

Combine all ingredients in a bowl and mix well. Brush on lamb frequently during the last 30 minutes of baking.

Barbara Schilde, Hahnville, Louisiana

INDEX

PHOTOGRAPHY CREDITS: Spanish Green Olive Commission; Pickle Packers International; National Macaroni Institute; California Strawberry Advisory Board; National Kraut Packers Association; Brussels Sprouts Marketing Program; National Cherry Growers and Industries Foundation; California Beef Council; Pet Milk Company; American Lamb Council; Anderson Clayton Company: Seven Seas Dressing; American Spice Trade Association; Florida Fresh Fruit and Vegetable Association; American Home Foods: Chef Boy-ar-Dee; Angostura-Wuppermann Corporation; Quaker Oats; Olive Administrative Committee; Louisiana Yam Commission; Peter Pan Peanut Butter; The R. T. French Company; Campbell Soup Company; Evaporated Milk Association; United Fresh Fruit and Vegetable Association; The Pillsbury Company; Processed Apples Institute; Southeastern Peanut Growers; Keith Thomas Company; National Dairy Council; Wheat Flour Institute; McIlhenny Company (Tobasco); Grandma's West Indies Molasses; California Foods Research Institute; Best Foods: A Division of Corn Products, International; Pie Filling Institute; California Raisin Advisory Board.

Printed in the United States of America.